GOD'S JESTERS

Humour from the Pulpit

Dennis McCloskey

Compiled by
Dennis McCloskey

Published by

Box 28, 1694B Burnstown Road
Burnstown, Ontario, Canada K0J 1G0
Telephone (613) 432–7697 or 1–800–465–6072

ISBN 1–894263–74–X
Printed and bound in Canada

Design and layout by Leanne Enright
Cover design by Bill Slavin
Printing by Custom Printers of Renfrew Ltd.

Canadian Cataloguing in Publication Data

God's jesters / (edited by) Dennis McCloskey

ISBN 1–894263–74-X

1. Catholic Church—Clergy—Humour. 2. Canadian wit and humour (English) I. McCloskey, Dennis, 1948-

PN6231.C5G63 2002 C818'.60208 C2002-905072-3

In memory
of the late Father Bill Harding,
one of the all-time great jesters of God.

CONTENTS

INTRODUCTION

CANADIANS ARE a funny lot.

But don't just take my word for it. On November 26, 2001, I read an IPSOS Reid poll that found that 99% of Canadians believe laughter is good for the health. Seven months later, on the occasion of Canada's 135th birthday on July 1, 2002, *The Toronto Star* published an editorial that stated one of the most endearing qualities of Canadians is our sense of humour. "Laughter has helped us keep our heads through the dark days in more than a century of nation building," the editorial pronounced. The writer noted that our first prime minister was a wit. Criticized once for his ministerial appointments, Sir John A. Macdonald shot back, "Give me better wood and I will give you a better cabinet."

I had been planning to publish a humour book for over a year. Just for the health of it. And when I learned there are 12,498,605 Roman Catholics in Canada, as well as 10,407 priests and 29,980 religious (nuns, brothers, monks), I decided to focus on something I've known ever since I was a young altar boy in the 1960s. Some priests are darn funny.

I have been inspired by the humour of the scores of Roman Catholic priests I have met on my life's journey. Priests like Father Bill Harding (see Chapter One) and my local Richmond Hill parish priest, Father Bill Scanlon (see Chapter Two). Some I've met on just a few occasions but have enjoyed their humour from afar. Like Father Philip Kennedy. My mother, Zoe, lives in Alliston, Ontario, and I occasionally accompany her to Mass at St. Paul the Apostle where Father Philip Kennedy was parish priest until he was transferred to a parish in Scarborough, Ontario. Father Kennedy always started a sermon with a joke. Here's one of his memorable ones:

> A young man took his non-Catholic girlfriend to Mass one Sunday. Since she did not understand what was going on during the service, he explained everything to her.
>
> When the priest arrived at the pulpit, the man explained to his girlfriend that the priest was now going to deliver the sermon.
>
> Before he spoke, the priest took off his watch, looked at it, and placed it before him on the lectern.
>
> The young woman leaned toward her boyfriend and whispered, "What does that mean?"
>
> "Nothing," replied the young man. "Absolutely nothing!"

Father Floyd Gallant of Rollo Bay, P.E.I., is another of the many priests with an abundance of good humour whom I've met. My late father, Waldo, and his family were baptized at Rollo Bay's St. Alexis Church even before the present-day large and graceful church was built in 1930, and I have been attending Mass there during summer vacations ever since I was a boy. A few years ago, I was sitting in the kitchen of my uncle Charlie's Bear River, P.E.I., home when Father Floyd walked in and joined in some local chatter, sports talk and much laughter. This is just one of the jokes he told that evening:

> The police in Montreal are stopping speeders and giving them tickets to a Montreal Canadiens hockey game. If motorists get caught speeding the second time, the police make them go to the game!

The late humorist Stephen Leacock said people will freely confess they have no ear for music, or no taste for fiction, or no interest in religion, but no one will admit they have no sense of humour. For those who think humour is a dangerous thing—especially when speaking of religion or the church—they should know that studies prove that people with a well-developed sense of humour are better at problem solving, are wiser in their handling of other people, and have a broader outlook on life.

Many of those people with a well-defined sense of humour can be found in the Catholic Church. They realize there is a crying need for laughter in the church and they know that humour can ease the approach to a sensitive or serious subject, that it influences people, and it helps to reduce conflict. And that's no joke.

One of those religious people who believe that humour is a gift to the human race is the Most Rev. Kenneth A. Angell, of the Diocese of Burlington, Vermont. Cardinal Angell is the brother of David Angell, who was killed, along with his wife, Lynn, during the September 11, 2001 terrorist attack on the World Trade Center in New York City. David was the creator and executive producer of the hit comedy TV show, *Frasier*. Two days after the horrendous act, Cardinal Angell spoke fondly of his brother, saying how wonderful it is to make people laugh. He said, "I am comforted when I think of the gift of laughter my brother brought to so many people."

Another member of the church hierarchy who is not afraid to show his lighter side from time to time—although others would say he is way too serious—is Aloysius Cardinal Ambrozic, Archbishop of Toronto. In 1998, the newly appointed cardinal was celebrating Mass at St. Michael's Cathedral in downtown Toronto. He said his appointment was put into perspective by his five-year-old grandniece, Chrissy, when she had overheard her parents talking about her grand-uncle's promotion to cardinal. The next day she went to school and told her classmates that he was going to become a robin!

I have heard priestly humour in the most unlikely places. On September 28, 1996, my wife and I attended a memorial service for one of our all-time favourite priests, Father Henri Nouwen, who died of a heart attack at the age of sixty-four while on his way to St. Petersburg, Russia, where Dutch Television was planning to film an adaptation of one of his many books, *The Prodigal Son.* Father Henri used to say the occasional Mass at our Richmond Hill church, and his sermons attracted standing room only crowds. (He was pastor at the nearby L'Arche Daybreak Community for people with developmental disabilities.) More than 1,000 people packed the Church of the Transfiguration in Markham, Ontario, for the funeral of this priest/philosopher/writer who was respected around the world. During the service, one of Father Henri's special friends from Daybreak stood on the altar and repeated Father Henri's favourite joke: *"How do you make holy water? You boil the hell out of it!"*

The priests I have known in my life have taught me (among other things) that humour and laughter is an exceedingly important part of human and spiritual life. This was true in the days of St. Thomas More (who possessed extraordinary good humour) and it is just as true in our broken world today. How do I know? The Bible tells me so. In Luke, Ch. 6, Vs. 20-21 it is written, *"Blessed are you that weep now, for you shall laugh."* And in the Book of Genesis Ch. 21, Vs. 6, Sarah said, *"God has made me laugh . . ."* Check out Psalms Ch. 2, Vs. 3, where it is written, *"He that dwelleth in Heaven shall laugh . . ."*

Even modern-day writers acknowledge that over the centuries the innocent laughter provided by witty, insightful anecdotes on the themes of religion, religious customs, and religious people—especially clergy—has been good for religions and their followers. So wrote Tom Harpur, theologian and author, in *The Toronto Star*, June 10, 2002. He added, "Christ laced parables with humour, but some of the fun is lost in translation." He also confirmed what many of us realize: that "levity, at the right time and place, can be a sign of wellness and a promoter of health."

Who among us is not aware of the joyous good humour of Pope John Paul II? In an Apostolic Letter in 2000 entitled *Novo Millennio Ineunte,* His Holiness wrote of the uniqueness of children who are made in the image of God. "All have the right to grow healthy and strong, to study, to play, to laugh. All children have the right to be children."

His words took on a new meaning for me during his World Youth Day (WYD) tour of Toronto in July 2002, when he captured the hearts of the world's youth. When he spoke to them on July 25 at Exhibition Place, he told them they could be young for the rest of their lives. I believe he was speaking to all of us. Why shouldn't we retain our child-like zest for life and humour for all of our lives? On July 26, His Holiness had lunch with fourteen WYD youths at a retreat on Strawberry Island, north of Toronto. One of the chosen few, seventeen-year-old Mamid, said, "We had lots of laughs." Reporting on the luncheon for *The Toronto Star*, Leslie Scrivener, Faith and Ethics Reporter, said, "It may be difficult to see the eighty-two-year-old pope—known as a philosopher, mystic, unbending moral authority and head of the world's one billion Roman Catholics—as a jokester, but several of his guests described him that way."

Early in 2002, in a bold gesture, I wrote to the pope and asked if he would consider submitting a favourite humorous story to my book. Not surprisingly, he declined, through an emissary, but in a letter from the Vatican Secretary of State's office, Monsignor Pedro Lopez Quintana said he appreciated my "sentiments" and added that "His Holiness will remember you in his prayers, and he invokes upon you God's abundant blessings."

Okay, so the pope didn't contribute directly to this book. But scores of Canadian Catholic priests from every province in the country answered my plea when I took up a collection for contributions of a favourite joke, humorous story or anecdote. To be honest, my request got a mixed reaction. Some ignored my request for submissions. A few invited me into their living rooms where we whiled away the time, sharing favourite jokes. A few e-mailed their favourite one-liners to me. One priest sent me twenty-seven pages of his favourite jokes; another sent twenty-four pages. One well-known Father had his assistant write to me saying he was unable to fulfil my request at this time because, "In his words, he is 'pathologically over-extended.'"

Now, there's a priest who needs to lighten up! Maybe I'll send him a copy of *God's Jesters!*

ACKNOWLEDGEMENTS

DURING MY writing career, which has spanned thirty-one years, I have published many articles about the humour of Catholic priests, so I had some grist for the mill even before I started this book. But I couldn't have put it all together without the help and co-operation of dozens and dozens of priests from Newfoundland & Labrador to British Columbia who contributed their favourite jokes and humour stories to this book. In appreciation of their bountiful stories, the publisher and I have made a financial contribution to two Roman Catholic charities in Canada.

I had intended to publish only church and religious-related jokes, but when priests indicated their humour was universal, I threw caution to the winds and accepted all forms of humorous stories and jokes. Then, reporter Susy Passos wrote a full-page article about my book project in the March 24, 2002 edition of *The Catholic Register*. Soon, I started hearing from strangers across the country who wanted to contribute a funny story about the church, religion, or the clergy. In a few cases, readers steered me to priests who were known for their joke telling. I also heard from friends, relatives, colleagues and Internet buddies who sent me jokes they thought would be suitable for the book.

Susy's article was entitled, "Hey Father, Have You Heard the One About . . .?" She began the story by noting, "There are books on lawyer jokes and books on doctor jokes, but has anyone heard of a book about priest's jokes?" She added, "That's a void that Dennis McCloskey wants to fill." As Susy reported, I merely want to show people another side of Roman Catholic priests—their funny side. I hope you'll agree with me that many of them do indeed have a wonderful sense of humour.

A few people tried to discourage me from publishing this book, citing the sexual abuse scandals in the church. I believe, however, the shameful sins of a few should not tarnish the good of the majority. I was determined not to let a small number of misguided priests and their misconduct take away from thc goodness and good humour of the vast majority of clerics in this country. The pope, in his WYD homily on July 28 in Downsview, Ontario, told 800,000 pilgrims not to be discouraged by the sins and failings of some of the Church's members. He encouraged them to "think of the vast majority of dedicated and generous priests and religious whose only wish is to serve and do good."

I received encouragement on many other fronts. A writing colleague in Regina wrote to me, saying, "Your book of priest's jokes is seriously a GREAT idea."

When I have an idea I want to develop, I am persistent and dogged in my determination to achieve my goal. Perhaps I can best explain this fortitude in a joke about a persistent duck. It was told to me on Friday, May 31, 2002, by Fred McEvoy, an Ottawa freelance writer/researcher. (Fred revealed to me that he had wanted to be a priest but, for a variety of reasons, became a periodical writer instead.) On this May evening Fred and I were enjoying a seafood dinner at Peake's Quay Restaurant, in Charlottetown, Prince Edward Island, the province of my birth (otherwise known as "God's Million Acre Farm"). Fred told what some people might consider the unfunniest joke ever. That may be so, but it speaks to me in volumes and it quacks me up every time I tell it:

> A duck went into a store and asked the storekeeper, "Do you have any duck food?"
>
> The storekeeper said, "No, we're all out of duck food."
>
> The duck left the store and returned the next day. "Do you have any duck food?" he asked the same storekeeper.
>
> "I told you yesterday, we're all out of duck food."
>
> The duck left and came back a day later. He asked the same question.
>
> The storekeeper became angry. "I told you yesterday and the day before, we don't have any duck food. If you ask me one more time, I will nail your webbed feet to the floor!"
>
> The next day, the duck returned and asked, "Do you have any nails?"
>
> The storekeeper said, "No, sorry, we're all out of nails."
>
> The duck asked, "Do you have any duck food?"

Dennis McCloskey
Fall, 2002

CHAPTER ONE

In all thy humours, whether grave or mellow,
Thou'rt such a touchy, testy, pleasant fellow;
Hast so much wit, and mirth, and spleen about thee,
There is no living with thee, nor without thee.

Joseph Addison

Father Bill Harding

May 14, 1923–September 12, 1994
North York, Ontario

I FIRST met Father William (Bill) Harding in 1967, and I must confess (no pun intended) that I soon became hooked on his never-ending supply of quips, anecdotes and one-liners. Nearly thirty years later, I wrote an article about my "humour mentor" that was published by Rev. F.J. Power, Editor of *Canadian Messenger Magazine*, in the April 1996 edition of his magazine. (One of Father Power's favourite jokes appears in this book, so now I've returned the favour.) I wrote the article, entitled "Heavenly Humour," because Father Bill Harding is the priest who had the greatest influence on my life. It is for that reason that I also dedicated this book to his memory.

His brother, Father Dave Harding, who's been a priest for more than sixty years, comes a close second in my Top Ten list of favourite priests. Father Dave acted as my "unpaid expert consultant" on this project. He and his brother Bill were inseparable throughout their lives and careers as priests. And I'd like you to meet them in this book because they are the wittiest people you'll ever meet.

One day, while I was putting the book together, I received an e-mail from Rev. Msgr. John Murphy, of Toronto, who told me of his friendship with Father Bill. "There are lots of fantastic jokes told from the pulpits of the land, and I enjoyed Father Bill's wit and humour on many occasions," he wrote. "I can hardly wait to meet up with him in the next life and hear his latest jokes."

During his homily at the Mass of the Resurrection for Father Bill, on September 15, 1994, then Father John Murphy said his friend was on his way to the Lord's Mountain where, as Isaiah told us, "the Lord has prepared a banquet of rich food."

"I hope and pray there is a golf course on the way to that mountain," Father Murphy told the gathering. "If there is, I am sure Father Bill has already played eighteen holes." He added, "If he now lives life in its fullest, he would want us to live life to its fullest . . . in Faith, Goodness, Joy, Peace, Laughter, and Holiness, we are confident that Father Bill, who has gone from us to God, goes no further from us than God. And God is very near."

Father Bill is introduced near the front of *God's Jesters* while Father Dave's baptism of jokes, and his thoughts on humour, appear at the back of the book. I did this consciously because these priests were like a matching pair of bookends for their entire lives. Two peas in a pod. Birds of a feather. They are, without doubt, two of a kind, and the mould was broken when they were made.

I've also written about them in other newspapers and publications, including *The Toronto Star* ("The Favourite Jokes of Well-Known Folks," *Toronto Star*, 1981), and *Good Times Magazine*. Father Dave was the "Merchant of Faith and Mirth" in that article published in January 2000. It is reprinted near the end of this book.

I began one of my recent articles about Father Bill by repeating Mark Twain's comment that there is no humour in heaven. I said that may have been the case in Twain's day but now that Father William F. Harding—the funniest priest this side of the Mississippi River—had passed on, the roll of thunder we heard from above the day he died was the sound of an appreciative audience rolling in the celestial aisles.

Father Bill was pastor at Prince of Peace Catholic Church in Scarborough, Ontario, until his death at age seventy-one. Since the witty cleric has had a captive audience beyond the pearly gates for more than eight years, I have no doubt that the "twain" have met and the late, great, American humorist has changed his punchline. He might also agree that he has met his match. God knows, with the likes of Mark Twain and Father Harding, it must be a laugh a minute up there!

When I first met this true Jester of God in 1967, he was serving as the pastoral wit at Toronto's Annunciation Church. He'd had the church built five years earlier and it became his cathedral of comedy. I was a newcomer to the city and I gravitated to his magnetism and humour. He had a repertoire of so many old, stolen jokes it would take a bishop to forgive such thievery. While the pulpit was Father Bill's stage, I sometimes arrived late for Mass only to be corralled at the back of the church to serve as a one-person audience for Father Bill's latest "warmed-over cabbage," while his brother, Father Dave, or another visiting priest celebrated Mass at the altar.

More often than not, he repeated the joke, story or one-liner that had appeared in that Sunday's bulletin under the heading "Laugh Here." He said he published a weekly joke because it was the best way to get his parishioners—both young and old—to read the other announcements. But he also said he hoped that the jokes "lifted their spirits, brightened their lives, calmed their fears, soothed their loneliness, enlightened their thinking, enriched their friendships, and tickled their funny bone."

He once compiled his collection of jokes and one-liners in a forty-four-page soft-cover book called *Har-Dee-Har-Har by Harding*. In his introduction, he wrote that the secret of happiness is in being able to see humour in the commonplace. "This is a rare gift," he wrote. "But it can be developed by having a happy outlook and attitude in your personal lifestyle." He acknowledged that many a true word is spoken in jest because "not only does a good joke or a funny story make us happy, it teaches us something important at the same time."

Here are some of the jokes he published in the booklet under the heading "Divine Light":

> THE LOCAL priest met one of his parishioners in the shopping plaza on a Monday morning. The parishioner said, "That was a damn fine sermon you preached yesterday, Father."
>
> "Thank you," said the priest. "But you shouldn't use language like that."
>
> "I'm sorry, Father," said the parishioner. "But it was such a damn fine sermon that I put a $100 bill in the collection plate."
>
> "The hell you did!" said the priest.

> A PRIEST who was preaching, shouted out the words of an apostle, "And what shall I say next?"
>
> Voice from the congregation: "Amen."

> PRIEST: "And what passage did you like best in my sermon?"
>
> PARISHIONER: "The one leading from the pulpit to the sacristy."

> TWO WOMEN who wanted to become Catholics were comparing their progress following an R.C.I.A. class one evening.
>
> One said, "I've gotten to Original Sin. Have far have you got?"
>
> Her friend replied, "Oh, I'm way beyond redemption."

> A ROMAN CATHOLIC missionary priest met a cannibal in an African jungle and asked, "Have you and your people ever heard of our religion?"
>
> "Oh, yes," said the cannibal. "We had a taste of it the last time a Jesuit came through here."

EPITAPH ON a gravestone:
"Pause stranger, as you pass me by;
As you are now, so once was I.
As I am now, so once you'll be;
So trust in God and follow me."

Underneath, someone wrote, "To follow you I'm not content, until I know which way you went."

I should make it clear now that Father Bill wasn't a wisecracking, motor-mouth gagster, the kind you pay to see at a comedy cabaret. This clerical comic had a serious side: In forty-six years as a curate and pastor he earned a PhD and published instructional books on such topics as training lay ministers and parenting. (He loved to say that parents spend the first three years of their children's lives trying to teach them to talk, and the next sixteen years trying to get them to shut up.)

He served in six parishes and was founding pastor of Annunciation in Don Mills, and Prince of Peace in Scarborough. He obtained his BA and Master of Education from the University of Toronto, a Master of Arts and Education from Niagara University, and a PhD from a university in California; and he was a licensed pilot.

His influence on my life, and that of my family, was profound. He not only officiated at my 1975 marriage to my wife, Kris, and at the marriages of my two sisters, he also influenced each of our spouses to embrace the Catholic religion in the 1960s and '70s.

He even helped me in my work. When I was a young corporate newsletter editor in the early 1970s, I relied on Father Bill's wit to fill the occasional glaring white space in my layout. I was writing articles for the brewing industry, so I sometimes borrowed gags from *Har-Dee-Har-Har*, lifting such groaners as, "When God gave out ears, I thought He said beers, so I asked for two big ones." And when I published my own 170-page book of beer quotes (*Mug Shots*, 1993), I attributed a few familiar *bon mots* to Father Bill, such as: "When God gave out legs, I thought He said kegs, so I asked for two fat ones."

It was also Mark Twain who said, "We are the only animal that blushes. Or needs to." I've seen Father Bill create a fire-red glow in a pale face, but when he laughed, his world laughed with him. Some may remember him best as a tenacious tennis player, others fondly recall this Irish tenor's rendition of "Danny Boy"; but I will forever cherish the memory of his wonderful wit.

In 1981, I was collecting the favourite jokes of famous Canadians for a freelance writing project that I was working on, so I asked him for a pet quip. He submitted an old familiar one, which I included in a feature that I sold to

The Toronto Star. Along with the published jokes of twenty well-known politicians, entertainers, artists, and business people, appeared Father Bill's contribution, which was the one about a priest in the pulpit who warned his congregation that every person in the parish would die someday. When a man in the front pew started to snicker, the priest asked what he was laughing about. The man replied, "I don't belong to this parish."

It's that kind of har-dee-har humour that endeared Father Bill to people, in part because some straitlaced Christians don't necessarily expect jocularity from a man of the cloth, but also because he was just so darned entertaining. If music is the laughter of life, this punny padre was a complete orchestra. He had an inextinguishable laugh and a charm that just wouldn't quit.

Comedian Sid Caesar once lamented the "loss of humanity" in modern humour. He said, in an interview with Knight Ridder newspapers, "This country is losing its sense of humour very fast." I don't think he was kidding. I suspect there's a ring of truth to what he says when we consider the state of the planet that's fraught with violent crime, fear of terrorist attacks, debt crises, unemployment, famine, wars, threat of nuclear war and proliferation of weapons of mass destruction, and other natural and man-made disasters. One could argue there's not much to laugh about these days.

Even priests, who have come under attack and much criticism in the past few years, could be excused for displaying a lack of mirth in a mirth-less society. But, to me, it seems they're a happier lot than the rest of us mortals. At least, the ones I know are. Perhaps they don't take life as seriously as the rest of us, because there's absolutely no question in their minds that there's a better life in the great beyond. If that's the case, they must reason, why not treat life as a joke that's just begun? Wouldn't it be great if our clergy actually end up being our saviours—through humour?

The last time I saw Father Bill Harding was in the spring of 1994. My father, who loved Father Bill dearly, was dying of cancer. One Sunday in March, I visited my humour mentor in his tiny church office in Scarborough and even in my grief he lightened my burden with stories about his recent golfing holiday in Vancouver. I laughed at his joke about bringing an extra pair of socks in case he got a hole in one.

It was that kind of kooky humour that made me laugh more than three decades ago, and later helped me smile through my tears at the time of my father's death. Father Bill hadn't changed. He'd gotten funnier. Like always, if he wanted to share a slightly off-colour joke, he'd tell it in a conspiratorial whisper, as though it were between just the two of us. But you knew he'd used that harmless line a hundred times before.

During my dad's illness, Father Bill phoned and voice-mailed and faxed me often to inquire about his condition. I would tell him that his body is weak but his sense of humour remains strong. When Dad died on Easter Sunday, surrounded by family, I called Father Bill and he said simply, "Thank God." I knew what he meant: "The suffering is over."

They say he who laughs last laughs best. Father Bill's laughter was silenced for the last time when he passed away five months later, following a stroke. Now he and my father are buried in the same cemetery at Holy Cross in Thornhill. I live nearby and often visit the 145-acre "garden of beauty and love."

Sometimes I think of Woody Allen's comment, "Our greatest fear is that there is an afterlife but no one will know where it's being held." Father Bill would have loved that line. He once told me the church he built at Prince of Peace Parish in 1987 has seating for nearly 1,000. "But with standing room, I can cram in 1,200 people to listen to my corny jokes," he said in his self-deprecating manner.

Now his audience is much bigger. And if God has a sense of humour, it's about time He appointed Father Bill Harding the Patron Saint of Joke-Tellers. Father Bill would love that because the laughs would be on him for eternity.

I suggest, if you're looking for heaven, just follow the laughter.

CHAPTER TWO

A person without a sense of humour is like a wagon without springs—jolted by every pebble on the road.

Henry Beecher

Father Bill Scanlon

St. Mary Immaculate Parish
Richmond Hill, Ontario

"If people don't want to come to church, nobody's going to stop 'em."

Variation on a quote by Yogi Berra

Father Bill Scanlon is a humorist, quipster, gagster and a wonderful, witty wisecracker. He didn't utter the Yogi Berra quote, but he would have if he'd thought of it first. It's this kind of rascally comment that Father Bill's parishioners have come to expect and enjoy throughout his several decades as a priest.

I met him thirty-two years ago when I was a journalism student at Ryerson, in Toronto. As sports editor of the *Daily Ryersonian* student newspaper, I assigned myself to cover a Flying Fathers charity hockey game one evening at Varsity Arena. The group of Catholic priests was (and still is) well known for breaking the stereotypical image of the solemn, straitlaced priest as they romped and goofed around on the ice to entertain the fans and raise money for charity. As an added bonus, the hockey was pretty darn good!

On this particular night, the opponents were the St. Michael's Oldtimers, who had a strong roster of former NHLers, such as Gus Mortson, Bill Colvin, Paul Knox and former Boston Bruin Leo Labine. Father Bill's team included Father Les Costello, a former St. Mike's junior player who also played in the NHL with the Toronto Maple Leafs. (Father Costello is currently parish priest at Saint Alphonsus in Schumacher, Ontario.) Costello was the best player on the ice that night but Father Bill was undoubtedly the most popular, as a group of fanatical youngsters in the crowd of 450 constantly chanted, "Father Bill! Father Bill!" followed by the Woody Woodpecker cackle.

In the dressing room after the game, Father Bill said he was a little disappointed at the turnout of a few hundred fans for the game (the largest crowd at a Flying Father's hockey game was 15,396 at Vancouver, B.C.), but he said it was more fun than playing bingo. As he sipped on a bottle of "wobbly pop" he facetiously proclaimed the team's philosophy, "Win or lose, hit the booze!" The comment is definitely tongue-in-cheek, for over the years the Flying Fathers have played more than 900 hockey games and they've won just about all of them. Millions of fans have witnessed their on-ice antics since their first game in 1962. In one game alone, in Toronto, they raised $240,000. Along the way, both fans and players have had a lot of fun. The Flying Fathers' theme song includes this refrain:

We play the game of hockey
And prove to everyone
That you can have religion
And still have some fun.

We're playing and we're praying
And we're doing what we should
Even when we give out checks
We give out brotherhood . . .

We always try to pull a stunt
To score those winning goals
And even when we lose the game
We still have won some souls!

As happens to most journalists after a story is published, I lost contact with Father Bill Scanlon but was pleasantly surprised to learn one day, many years ago, that he was being transferred from his Newmarket parish to the church I attend regularly in Richmond Hill. I soon got an indication of what was to come, in terms of levity, when I mentioned to a colleague (Joe Scanlon) the name of our new priest. "Oh, Father Bill. That's my uncle," he said. "He doesn't like to work on Sundays."

The jokes haven't stopped. They just keep on coming. There may be one or two parishioners who don't fully appreciate Bill Scanlon's dry wit or ironic humour, but they are few and far between. Most of us recognize that his love of sports, and his affection for humour and laughter is his way of allowing some light to shine on the world.

Obviously he's a very dedicated priest, first and foremost, but if there were an Olympics for Clerical Humour, Father Bill would certainly be on the medals podium. Much of his humour-from-the-altar involves sports: February 3, 2002 was Super Bowl Sunday, and his sermon touched on the theme of attitude. "I've got the right attitude today," he announced from the pulpit. "I'm betting the collection on the St. Louis Rams." (Turns out the underdog New England Patriots defeated the once-mighty Rams 20–17.)

As an aside, he recognized that Super Bowl XXXVI could cause a lot of stress in some households. "Some people recommend that the best way to deal with stress is to follow the directions on the bottle of that well-known headache remedy," Father Bill suggested. "Take two aspirins and keep away from children."

Some funny people use humour to hide pain while others use it to hammer home a message. It's clear that Father Bill belongs to the latter category of humorist. During his sermon on April 28, 2002, he told the congregation about his fairly recent double knee replacement operation. He told us about the many specialists who had helped him to "know the way" prior to his surgery by explaining in detail what medical procedures would be done. "In my case, most of the specialists were psychiatrists," he joked, before adding that he had donated his own blood for the operation "so as not to mix the blood alcohol content." He continued to crack jokes about returning to the rectory after the operation and asking Associate Pastor Father Simon DeGale to anoint him "because I didn't have a leg to stand on."

His self-deprecating comments that Sunday brought peals of laughter from the congregation, but the point he was making was not lost on them either, because everyone knows that a double knee transplant is not a walk around the block. The gospel reading that day was from John 14:1–12, in which Jesus said to his disciples, *"Do not let your hearts be troubled. Believe in God, believe also in me. In my Father's house, there are so many dwelling places. If it were not so, would I have told you that I go to prepare a place for you?"* In his own inimitable style, Father Bill was letting us know that he was a little bit worried about the outcome of the operation. (He has been a superb sportsman all his life and isn't ready to hang up the skis yet.) Later in the reading, Thomas says, *"Lord, we do not know where you are going. How can we know the way?" Jesus said to him, "I am the way, and the truth, and the life. No one comes to the Father except through me. If you know me, you will know my Father also. From now on you do know him and have seen him."*

If there is a defining characteristic that best describes Father Bill Scanlon, it is his love of sports. His favourite place in winter is a chalet in Collingwood, Ontario, near the hills of Blue Mountain. And he loves to share his sporting stories from the pulpit. At the 8:15 a.m. Mass on April 14, 2002, he said he'd been skiing the previous weekend and "closed down the mountain" when the lifts stopped running at 4:30 p.m. It happened to be the last day the ski resort would be operating before shutting down for the season. The chair lift operator, who is familiar with the skiing priest, bade him farewell, saying, "See you next year, Reverend. Happy pasturing." As he told the story to his flock at St. Mary Immaculate, Father Bill chuckled and said he had a vision of himself standing in a field with a herd of Holsteins.

On that same day on the ski hills of Collingwood, he was chatting with three regular skiers. One said to him, "Father, we never go to church, but when you're skiing behind us, we pray a lot!"

With most joke tellers, it's easy to separate the wheat from the chaff. But Father Bill's infectious humour is so finely honed and honest-to-God natural, it doesn't matter if he's embellishing a story to make us laugh. And he doesn't have to venture very far to find a humorous tale. At one time, there was a telephone installed on the wall of the upper choir loft at St. Mary Immaculate. When a young boy asked Father Bill why there was a phone in the choir loft, the lad received this answer: "When the choir director notices that the priest on the altar is getting tired, he calls down to the sacristy to tell them to warm up another priest."

Long-time churchgoers at St. Mary are accustomed to the wit and wisdom of their parish priest, and it's clear that the mood he sets is picked up pretty quickly—even by visiting priests. On June 23, 2002, Father Noel Sanvicente spoke to the congregation at the Sunday Masses during his visit to North America to seek financial support (and prayers) for his missionary parish in the Diocese of Cabanatuan, Philippines. He started his appeal by telling us that Father Bill had given him the following advice: "Talk less and they will give more."

Amid the chuckles, Father Noel added to the light tone by explaining that there are some 7,100 islands in the Philippines, "depending on whether it's low tide or high tide." As part of his introduction, Father Noel said his parents bestowed the Christmas moniker on him because his mother was forty-two years old when he was born, and he was thus considered "a gift from God." At the end of the Mass, Father Bill thanked Father Noel for visiting St. Mary. "My mother was also forty-two when I was born," he told the worshippers. "However, I don't think she considered me a gift from God. Apparently she cried out, 'It's just another Bill.'"

In thanking Father Noel for his fundraising efforts, Father Bill seized the opportunity to end the service with a story about a woman who once greeted him at the back of the church by asking what he had done with the money. "I was taken by surprise but I didn't want to commit myself so I asked her what money she was talking about," he said. The woman replied: "The money your mother gave you for singing lessons!"

As I mentioned earlier, there is often a valid point to his priestly humour. February 17, 2002 was the first Sunday in Lent, and in his sermon Father Bill spoke of the sin of temptation. He alluded to the first reading (Gen. 2:7–9, 16–18, 25; 3:1–7), which reads, in part, *"And the Lord God commanded the man, 'You may freely eat of every tree of the garden; but of the tree of the knowledge of good and evil you shall not eat, for in the day that you eat of it you shall die.'"*

True to form, he related a story about temptation. He told of a young associate priest who never got to give the homily. The older priest always preached the sermon. The months went by and the young priest was becoming increasingly frustrated. One day, he wondered what would happen if he tore a leaf from the old priest's written homily. The following Sunday, he succumbed to the temptation and ripped a leaf from the pastor's prepared sermon. At the appointed time in the Mass, the stodgy veteran priest made his way to the pulpit and began to deliver his sermon. Midway through his talk, the churchgoers heard the following: *". . . and Adam says to Eve . . . hmmm . . . a leaf is missing."*

I truly believe that the vast majority of St. Mary's faithful enjoy and relish Father Bill's humour. But even if a few do not, it doesn't stop him from having fun with them. His constant companion is a beautiful, brown Labrador named Peppy, who often accompanies Father Bill and the other celebrants at the altar during Mass. One woman was quite upset to see a dog at the altar, and voiced her displeasure to Father Bill one winter's day. The appearance of the donkeys and cows and sheep in the nearby manger didn't seem to have drawn the woman's scorn, as she huffed, "If you can bring your dog to church, then I can bring my cat." Father Bill responded to the threat with customary wit, "That would be great! Peppy would love that! He could have your cat for lunch." *(Editor's note: Please see the section of this book about P.E.I.'s Father Leo Trainor and his dog, Ranger, the only dog in Canada banned by the bishop from attending Mass.)* As you can tell by now, I could go on and on about the light-hearted reputation of Father Bill Scanlon. Let me just dig into my pile of Scanlon stories and leave you with one more of his self-admittedly recycled jokes:

> A Scottish atheist was in a boat, fishing. All of a sudden, the Loch Ness monster rose out of the water and thrust the boat and the fisherman high into the air, with one swish of its gigantic tail.
>
> Mid-point in the sky, just as he was about to fall into the gaping jaws of the monster, the man yelled, "God, help me!"
>
> A voice came from above. "But I thought you didn't believe in me."
>
> The fisherman cried, "Aw, c'mon, God. Give me a break. Until a minute ago, I didn't believe in the Loch Ness monster, either!"

CHAPTER THREE

"Life is God's joke on us. It's our mission to figure out the punch line."
John Guarrine

Father Gerry Ward

St. Timothy Parish
Winnipeg, Manitoba

Father Ward is an Irishman who said that a book about God's Jesters is a great idea. He admits to a historical preference to stories about older priests who are stuck in their ways and who totally rely on their housekeeper. Whenever Father Ward goes to a new parish, this is the story he always tells:

> FATHER'S HOUSEKEEPER, Brigid, was in charge of all his appointments. If Brigid didn't like you, it might take you some time to get to see Father.
>
> She dictated the breakfast time and what Father would eat. She also planned and prepared the menu for lunch and dinner, as well as the hour he would eat it. Father was quite complacent and always went along with Brigid's plans. One year, for the annual priest's retreat, the bishop brought in a psychologist to address "The Power of the Irish Priest's Housekeeper and How to Undermine It." Upon his return from the weeklong retreat, Father entered the house by the front door. There was Brigid down on her hands and knees just finishing the waxing of the linoleum. "Away round to the back door with you," she yelled to Father. "Can't you see I've just finished the floor?"
>
> Father stamped down the length of the hall towards Brigid, stood over her and said, "Let me tell you what I learned this week at the retreat. First, I will decide what time breakfast is, and what I would like to eat for breakfast; the same applies to the other meals. And, I will go to bed when I choose, take over my appointment book and see whomever I please, whenever I please." Then he added triumphantly," What do you think of that, my girl?"
>
> Brigid fixed him with a steely stare and said, "That's the last retreat you're going on!"

Father Wayne L. Lobsinger

Holy Cross Parish

Georgetown, Ontario

ONE EVENING, an elderly priest decided to take a walk. During his walk, he heard a small voice calling, "Help me, help me!" He looked all around but saw nothing.

He continued to stroll, and again he heard a small voice, "Help me, help me!" He looked around once again and saw a little frog. He realized, to his astonishment, it was the frog calling for help. He bent over and picked up the frog.

As the elderly priest stared at the frog, it began to speak. "I am actually a beautiful princess. If you kiss me, I will turn back into a beautiful princess and I will kiss you and hug you and love you forever."

The priest thought for a moment, put the frog in his coat pocket and continued on his walk.

The frog popped its head out of the pocket and asked, "What's the matter? Aren't you going to kiss me?"

The elderly priest replied, "Frankly, at this stage of my life, I'd rather have a talking frog."

Father Harold O'Neill

Church of St. Gregory the Great

Picton, Ontario

There are approximately 1,365 parishioners at Picton's Church of St. Gregory the Great, at #7 Church Street, but Father O'Neill is also responsible for the mission church at nearby Wellington, where, as you will see, things are quite folksy:

ONE SUNDAY morning, when I arrived from Picton at our little mission church of St. Frances in Wellington, several parishioners were already waiting for me in the brilliant sunshine.

As I rushed toward the narrow gate at the entrance of the church, Mr. and Mrs. Creamer and their four-year-old granddaughter, Virginia, greeted me. Mrs. Creamer handed me a jar of her homemade strawberry jam. I thanked her and took the jam into the sacristy with me.

Half an hour later, as Clarence and Nellie Creamer returned to their pew after receiving Holy Communion, the whole congregation heard Virginia ask, "Did he have the jam on it yet?"

Father Paul J. Riley

Holy Rosary and St. Stephen Parishes

St. Stephen, New Brunswick

Father Paul Riley has a special place in my heart because, although he lives in New Brunswick, he is originally from Alberton, Prince Edward Island, which happens to be the tiny community in Western P.E.I. where I first saw the light of day on September 15, 1948, at Western Hospital.

Father Riley is pastor at two very old parishes: St. Stephen (founded 1887) and St. Stephen (1838)—but I won't go so far as to say his jokes are that old! He said he hopes this book will be a "big hit" and he kindly offered a few that he admitted he has used before:

THREE SONS left home, went out on their own and prospered. Years later, when they reunited, they discussed the gifts they were able to give their elderly mother.

The first said, "I built a big house for our mother."

The second said, "I sent her a Mercedes with a driver."

The third smiled and said, "I've got you both beat. You remember how mom enjoyed reading the Bible? And you know she can't see very well. I sent her a remarkable parrot that recites the entire Bible. It took parishioners in the church twelve years to teach him. He's one of a kind. Mama just has to name the chapter and verse, and the parrot recites it."

Soon thereafter, Mom sent out her letters of thanks. "Dear Milton," she wrote to one son. "The house you built is so huge. I live in only one room, but I have to clean the whole house."

"Dear Gerald," she wrote to another. "I am too old to travel. I stay at home most of the time, so I rarely use the Mercedes. And the driver is so rude!"

"Dearest Donald," she wrote to her third son. "You are the only one who has the good sense to know what your mother likes. The chicken was delicious."

A CAT died and went to heaven. God met him at the Gate and said, "You have been a good cat all of these years. Anything you desire is yours. All you have to do is ask."

The cat said, "Well, I lived all my life with a poor family on a farm and had to sleep on hardwood floors."

God took the hint. "Say no more." A fluffy pillow appeared instantly.

A few days later, six mice were killed in an accident and they went to heaven. God met them at the Gate with the same offer He gave the cat.

The mice said, "All our lives we've had to run. Cats, dogs and even women with brooms have chased us. If we could only have a pair of roller skates, we wouldn't have to run anymore."

God said, "Say no more." And instantly, each mouse was fitted with a beautiful pair of tiny roller skates.

A week later, God decided to see how the cat was doing. He found the cat sound asleep on his new pillow. God gently woke him and asked, "How are you doing? Are you happy here?"

The cat yawned, stretched and said, "Oh, I've never been happier in my life. And those Meals on Wheels you've been sending over are the best!"

A LITTLE boy was in a relative's wedding. As he walked down the aisle of the church, he would take two steps, stop, and turn to the crowd. While facing the people, he would put his hands up like claws and roar.

And so it went: step, step, ROAR, step, step, ROAR, all the way down the aisle.

The crowd was laughing hard by the time he reached the pulpit.

When asked what he was doing, the child said, "I was being the Ring Bear."

ONE SUNDAY morning after Mass, the priest noticed that little Alex was staring up at the large plaque that hung in the foyer of the church. It was covered with names, and small Canadian flags were mounted on either side of it.

The seven-year-old had been staring at the plaque for some time, so the priest approached the little boy and said quietly, "Good morning, Alex."

"Good morning, Father," replied the boy, still focused on the plaque. "Father McGhee, what is this?" he asked.

"Well, son, it's a memorial to all the young men and women who died in the service."

They stood together in silence, staring at the large plaque.

Little Alex's voice was barely audible when he asked, "Which service? The 9:00 or the 10:30?"

AN ELDERLY gentleman had serious hearing problems for a number of years. Finally, he went to the doctor, who was able to have him fitted for a set of hearing aids that allowed the gentleman to hear 100%.

A month later, the elderly gentleman returned to the doctor's office for a check-up. The doctor said, "Your hearing is perfect. Your family must be really pleased that you can hear again."

The gentleman said, "Oh, I haven't told my family, yet. I just sit around and listen to the conversations. In the last thirty days, I've changed my will three times!"

Father Charles T. Forget

St. John Vianney
Barrie, Ontario

More than 11,300 Roman Catholics belong to St. John Vianney Church in Barrie (and more in the mission church, Our Lady of the Assumption in Belle Ewart, for which Father Forget is also responsible), but it took a visitor to the Barrie church to steer me toward this clerical comic.

Maureen Jibb-Leeder and her husband are from Bracebridge, Ontario, and they attended the five p.m. Mass at St. John Vianney one Saturday evening when Father Forget led off his sermon by delivering two jokes. "We have been laughing over those jokes ever since," Maureen wrote in an e-mail.

When I contacted Father Forget and told him that I had heard from one of his "fans," he conceded that he had "loads of jokes" and admitted somewhat reluctantly that he seems to have a knack for remembering and telling jokes. "I rarely tell a joke just for the sake of giving people a laugh," he said. "For me, a joke is most useful to make a point in a homily. People love to laugh, especially in church where they are not accustomed to do so." He conceded that telling jokes is a fine and difficult art. "Sometimes a joke will offend, not because it was intended to offend or is offensive per se, but sometimes people are sensitive about certain things that have happened in their lifetimes and certain jokes can evoke sad or bad memories."

Father Forget thanked me for my sense of humour and proceeded to relay some of his favourites. The first two are the ones Maureen and her husband are still laughing over:

A MAN'S rather disagreeable wife died and a funeral was held for her in the church they had attended all their married lives.

Following the funeral service, as the pallbearers were carrying the casket through the main doors of the church, one of them stumbled and bumped the casket into the wall, jarring the lid. To everyone's shock and amazement a moan was heard, coming from inside the casket. When the lid was opened, it was discovered that the woman was still very much alive.

She lived for another ten years until she died again. Once more, there was a funeral in the church and following the service, as the pallbearers were about to exit through the main doors carrying the casket, her husband yelled out, "Watch out for the wall!"

A WOMAN boarded a city bus and saw a friend she had not seen for about a year. The two exchanged greetings and the woman sat in the seat beside her friend.

The first woman said, "I am so sorry to hear that your husband died about six months ago. What happened?"

Her friend said, "Well, he went quick. I was preparing dinner one evening and realized that I didn't have a vegetable for our meal, so I asked my husband to go out to the garden and pick a head of cabbage for me. While he was doing that, he suffered a massive heart attack and died on the spot, right there in the garden."

The woman said to her friend, "My God, that must have been awful! What did you do?"

Her friend replied, "Well, what could I do? I had to open a can of peas!"

IN A SMALL town with only one church, the parish priest was celebrating his birthday.

Three children of parishioners appeared at the rectory door to present Father with presents.

When he answered the door, each child, in turn, presented his or her gift with a prepared speech.

The first to present a gift was a little girl who said, "Here Father, this is for you. Happy birthday!" It was a small, flat, rectangular box, beautifully wrapped with gold paper and a bow. The parish priest knew that the little girl's mother owned the local candy store, so he said to the little girl, "Thank you so much for the box of chocolates."

Surprised, the little girl asked, "Father, how did you know it was a box of chocolates? You haven't even opened it yet!" The priest put a finger to his temple and replied, "Because Father knows everything!"

Next, a little boy moved forward to present his gift, which was in a much bigger box than the one containing the chocolates, and gave it to the priest with the same salutation. The priest received the gift and thanked the little boy, saying, "Thank you very much for the sweater." (The priest knew that the little boy's mother worked in the local clothing store.)

The boy was amazed. "Father, how did you know that it was a sweater—you haven't even opened it?"

Again, the priest answered, "Because Father knows everything!"

The last child to present her gift stepped up and thrust her wrapped gift into the priest's open hands. This gift was wrapped with brown parcel paper tied with a red ribbon and was much larger than the others. When the priest took it from the little girl he realized that the bottom of the present was damp. He expressed his gratitude to the little girl saying, "Thank you for the bottle of scotch." (The priest knew that the little girl's father ran the local liquor store.)

This time, however, to the priest's surprise, the little girl said, "No, Father, it isn't a bottle of scotch!"

"The priest placed a damp finger in his mouth, then asked, "Is it rye?"

"No!" said the little girl.

Again, tasting his finger, "Is it gin?" inquired the priest.

"No!" the little girl giggled. "I brought you a puppy!"

AN AGING monsignor was beginning to realize he was not able to remember as he once had.

This became evident one Sunday when he was preaching about the loaves and fishes. He began his homily by saying, "Today, we have just heard the gospel of the loaves and the fishes, when Jesus took five thousand loaves of bread and two thousand fish and he fed five people."

Suddenly, a man sitting in the front pew shouted out, "Monsignor, I could have done that!"

Monsignor was a bit thrown off by this remark, unaware of what he had said, but he continued on with his homily anyway. After Mass the monsignor was frustrated and angry at being heckled, and while speaking to the assistant priest he said, "Can you believe the nerve of that man, heckling me like that during my homily?" The assistant replied, nervously, "Well, Monsignor, you did kind of confuse things a bit."

"What do you mean?" questioned monsignor.

The assistant continued, "Well, actually you said that Jesus took five thousand loaves of bread and two thousand fish and that he fed only five people."

The monsignor's jaw dropped as he uttered, "I said that?"

"Yes, Monsignor, you did."

With resolve in his voice the monsignor asserted, "Then I'll just fix that in next Sunday's homily."

The following Sunday, during his homily, the monsignor attempted to set straight his verbal blunder of the previous Sunday. He began, "Last Sunday in my homily I mistakenly said that Jesus took five thousand loaves of bread and two thousand fish and he fed only five people. What I meant to say was that Jesus took five loaves of bread and two fish and he fed over five thousand people."

At this point, the same man sitting in the front row, stood up and exclaimed, "Monsignor, I could have done that!"

Monsignor had had enough. Looking straight into the eyes of the man who had spoken he asked, "You sir, how could you have done that?"

The man, now with a wide grin on his face, answered, "Simple. I'd just use the leftovers from last Sunday's homily!"

A YOUNG man named Paul wanted to marry a young woman whom he had been seeing for a year. Her name was Jennifer.

Being a sentimental kind of guy, Paul wanted to follow the old custom of asking permission of his girlfriend's father for his daughter's hand in marriage. So, one morning Paul went to Jennifer's dad and said, "Sir, I love your daughter. I would like to ask your permission to marry her."

Jennifer's father was touched by this gesture and liked Paul very much, so he said, "Paul, you are a good man. My wife and I really think a lot of you. You have my permission."

So, later that day Paul asked Jennifer to marry him. Overcome with emotion and with tears of joy, she accepted his proposal.

That evening, Jennifer told her father, "Dad, today Paul asked me to marry him, and I said yes." Jennifer began to sob.

Concerned about his daughter's emotional state, her father asked, "What's the matter, dear?"

Jennifer continued, "Well, Dad, I really love Paul and I want to marry him, but I don't know if I could ever leave Mom!"

Jennifer's father straightened up, placed his hand on his daughter's shoulder, looked her straight in the eye and said, "Honey, I love you very much. And I don't want anything to come between you and your happiness. You can take your mother with you!"

ON THE day that I was going to be installed in the parish of Saint John Vianney as pastor, the local bishop arrived to preside.

While I was in the vestry, getting ready for the occasion, one of the altar servers asked me, "So Father, does this mean you are going to be pastorized?"

ONE TIME, in my home parish of St. John the Evangelist, in Whitby, during the solemnity and silence of a Good Friday service, a little boy was acting up, causing much embarrassment to his father.

Finally, the man picked up his son and walked briskly down the main aisle to take his son outside, most likely for a severe reprimand.

Just as they were about to exit the church, the little boy yelled a single word, a plaintive cry that reverberated throughout the church:

"HELP!"

YEARS AGO, I attended an Ash Wednesday Mass at St. Michael's Cathedral in Toronto, with my aunt. She had multiple sclerosis, and at that time she was using a folding wheelchair because she could not walk long distances without getting tired.

In the cathedral, I helped her from her chair and into a pew, folded up the wheelchair, and placed it against the wall. When the ashes were being distributed to the congregation, I told my aunt that I would go up last and ask the priest to come back and give her ashes in her pew.

I took my place at the end of the line, and when finally it was my turn to receive my ashes, I blurted out my request, not realizing what I had said until I saw the priest trying to contain his laughter. Reflecting on my words, I realized I had said, "Father, my aunt has MS. Could you give her ashes on her seat, please?"

WHEN I was stationed at St. Patrick's in Markham, Ontario, there were two secretaries. One looked after the reception desk at the front of the office, and the other, who was the bookkeeper, used an office in the back.

One day, the bookkeeper and I were working at a computer in the back office, near the staff washroom, when the secretary from the front desk popped her head into the room. She intended to ask one of us to answer the phone if it rang, so she said, "I'm just going to the washroom. Would you guys listen for me?"

We looked at one another and burst out laughing.

Father Fred Monk

St. Mary's Church
Cochrane, Alberta

Father Monk recalled several incidents over the years "when one's tongue gets in the way while presiding at liturgy, reading the gospel, or singing." The following are some of his favourites:

IN THE late 1970s one of my brother priests was pastor in a small Alberta town. Father Greg has a powerful singing voice and often led the singing at Mass.

One Sunday he announced, "The closing hymn today will be number 325. The Mass is ended. All go in peace."

In his best, loudest and booming voice he led the congregation as he sang, "*The Ass is mended . . .*"

The congregation and Father Greg burst into laughter. It was the last time the parish ever used that hymn.

FATHER GREG is also well known for his Ash Wednesday Blooper:

As he raised his hand to bless the ashes, he proclaimed, in his best liturgical voice, "Lord, bless these asses by which we show that we are dust."

FATHER MARTIN Hagel, a dear friend who is now with the Lord, read the gospel one Sunday about the woman who had suffered from a hemorrhage for many years. A slip of the tongue caused him to read about the woman ". . . who suffered from hemorrhoids for many years."

IN THE old Lectionary, the Sunday readings were printed in order of the Sunday, or feast. For example, years AB&C for the 12th Sunday in Ordinary Time was printed under the title, "12th Sunday in Ordinary Time."

One Sunday a window was left open and the wind blew the page after the second reader had completed the reading. This was my fourth Mass that Sunday and I had already read the gospel three times. The reading was from the Gospel of Matthew and it began with, "And Jesus said to his Disciples . . ."

When I got up and began to read the gospel (not knowing the page had been "turned"), I immediately realized I was reading the wrong thing. The "wrong reading" also began with, "And Jesus said to his disciples . . ." I could hear parishioners paging through their missalettes to find the "right" reading. After the first sentence, I looked up at a smiling congregation, turned the page and said, "And in Year B, Jesus said to his disciples . . ."

This next story is told by Susan Duckett (mother of Matthew) and submitted by Father Fred Monk, Pastor, St. Mary's Church, Cochrane, Alberta.

ON A Sunday morning, our church parking lot and gathering area can be an intimidating place for a small child who becomes separated from his parents. Our son, Matthew, was in the habit of escaping from his parents and older siblings almost every Sunday.

This particular Sunday, when Matthew was about nine years old and when Father Fred Monk was assistant pastor, Matthew performed his magic escape routine as usual, but on this occasion he was lost for a considerable length of time.

We searched all the regular places and asked all our friends if they had spotted him.

After quite some time, the parking lot was almost empty and still no sign of Matthew. Then, with as little warning as his initial disappearance, Matthew appeared again at our side. "Matthew, where were you?" my husband and I called simultaneously.

"I was lost in the parking lot and God found me," he proclaimed loudly.

"God," as we found out later, was disguised as Father Fred Monk and he had indeed rescued Matthew from the hundreds of cars exiting from the parking lot. Father Fred "did not claim equality with God" but was nonetheless honoured to have been given such an exalted title.

Father Monk's response:

What lessons can we draw from this humorous story of one small boy with Down's syndrome and his encounter with God? First, in a small child's concrete mind, God is literally in the person of parents, priests, and those bigger than him. We must therefore strive to be that image of God. Second, all of us may at times become lost and have trouble finding God, but rest assured that God will always find us. "Rejoice with me; for I have found my sheep which was lost." Luke 15:6.

Father Gérald J. Croteau

Paroisse Ste-Cecile de Masham
La Pêche, Quebec

It was a particular delight to hear a Quebec priest say, "I think it's a wonderful idea to write this book." Father Croteau even offered to buy a copy when it's published. On top of all that, he submitted the following stories:

AS WE were preparing for the offering at one of our Mass celebrations, I turned to the altar servers. One of them was a boy who was new at this. I picked up the cruet of wine and poured it into the chalice.

The wine did not look like it usually does. So I swirled it, smelled it and wondered if the wine was okay. I decided to taste it. As I did, with all eyes of the congregation on me, I said aloud and into the portable microphone, "Maple syrup!"

There was a burst of laughter from the congregation and a puzzled look from the servers, especially the rookie server. I turned towards the faithful, looking for a culprit. One of the parishioners (who was a known prankster) objected to my looks and said with hands and mouth that he was not responsible for this.

We continued the Mass, with occasional giggles throughout. I asked the servers to get me another chalice and real wine.

After the most unusual Mass I have ever celebrated, the altar boy confessed that he mistakenly took the maple syrup bottle in the fridge for the wine bottle and filled the cruet. To this day, we do not keep maple syrup in the fridge.

JUNE 24 is St-Jean-Baptiste Day in Quebec, and it has been a legal holiday in that province since 1922.

On one particular June 24th, a colleague and I were visiting an English-speaking priest at St.Thomas Church in Campbellton, New Brunswick, and we were invited to celebrate Mass. My friend and I are French-speaking. The parish is English-speaking with English ritual books. "No problem," I said. "We'll translate as we go along."

We began to celebrate Mass, and things were going well until I got to the Epistle. It was a letter of Paul. I stood at the pulpit and started my translation: "*Paul a dit que* . . ." ("Paul said that . . .") and then I stumbled at the next word. And then the next . . . and so on.

The celebrant started laughing. I joined in the laughter.

We never celebrated another St-Jean-Baptiste Mass in French in an English parish.

Father Gérard Gauthier

St. John the Baptist Parish
Fort McMurray, Alberta

WHEN MY niece was three years old, I was visiting my folks when she came into the house. She looked at me and asked, "Are you a PRIEST?"

I replied, "Yes, I am a priest. Do you know what priests do?"

"SURE," she replied. "They sing LORD HAVE MERCY, and they talk LOUD."

AN ELDERLY man was dying at home and his wife was spending as much time as possible with him at his bedside, going back and forth from her household chores. He would lose consciousness and then come to for a while. At one lucid point, he opened his eyes to see her beside him.

He asked her, "What are you doing?"

"I am baking."

"What are you baking?"

"Butter tarts."

"Ahh, my favourite."

"I know—that is why I am baking them."

"Could I have one?"

"No, they are for the funeral."

Father Gerard Pettipas, C.Ss.R.

St. Joseph's Parish
Grande Prairie, Alberta

Father Pettipas and I are both former "armed forces brats" and although we lived with our families on many bases across Canada, we never met. When I asked him recently if he had any funny stories that he'd like to share, he responded by sending several pages of his "repertoire of jokes" that he uses on Cursillo Weekends. (One definition of the Cursillo Movement states, "The purpose or goal is to make Christian community possible in neighbourhoods, parishes, work situations, and other places where people live the greater part of their lives. It makes it possible for anyone in the world to live a Christian life in a natural way.")

Father Pettipas said he couldn't send me his best joke (about a camel) because it has to be performed. Another of his "better-to-be-performed jokes" is a dog-jaw story. (Okay, you have to be there!) He promised to "show" the jokes to me whenever we meet. Here's a small sampling of his repertoire:

A MIDDLE-aged woman had a heart attack and was taken to the hospital. While on the operating table she had a near-death experience. Seeing God, she asked, "Is my time up?"

God said, "No, you have another forty years, two months and eight days to live."

When she recovered, the woman decided to stay in the hospital and have a facelift, liposuction, and a tummy tuck. Since she had so much more time to live, she figured she might as well make the most of it. She even had someone come in and change her hair colour.

After a final bout of cosmetic surgery, she was released from the hospital. While crossing the street on her way home, she was run over and killed by a bus. When she arrived in front of God, she was angry. "I thought you said I had another forty years to live. Why didn't you pull me from the path of the bus?"

God replied, "Sorry, I didn't recognize you."

THREE STRINGS were going down the street, and wanted to drop into a bar for a drink.

They came to a tavern, and as they entered, one string said to his friends, "You get a table and I'll get the drinks."

"Bartender," he said, "I'd like some drinks for me and my friends."

"We don't serve strings in this place," said the bartender. Get out of here, the three of you!"

Confused and offended, they left the tavern.

A little further on, they came to a second watering hole. "Let's try in here," suggested one of the other strings. "But this time, let me try to get the drinks."

As he approached the bar, the bartender scowled at him. "Whaddya think you're doing in here, string? Get out, the lot of you, and don't think of coming back in here!"

They came upon yet another tavern. "This time, let me try," suggested the third string. But before he entered, he tied himself into a knot, and then frayed his hair. He stood at the bar, and with a firm voice declared, "Bartender, I'd like some drinks for me and my friends!"

The bartender studied his patron with a quizzical eye. "Hold on a minute! Aren't you a string?"

"No, I'm a frayed knot."

A KINDERGARTEN teacher was observing her classroom of children while they drew. She would occasionally walk around to see each child's artwork. When she got to one little girl who was working diligently, she asked what the drawing was.

The little girl replied, "I'm drawing God."

The teacher paused. "But no one knows what God looks like."

"They will in a minute."

A SUNDAY school teacher was discussing the Ten Commandments with her pre-school students. After explaining the commandment, *Honour thy father and thy mother*, she asked, "Is there a commandment that teaches us how to treat our brothers and sisters?"

Without missing a beat, one little boy answered, *"Thou shalt not kill."*

A LITTLE girl was watching her mother do the dishes at the kitchen sink. She noticed that her mother had several strands of white in her brunette hair.

The girl asked, "Why are some of your hairs white, Mommy?"

Her mother replied, "Well, every time you do something wrong to make your mother cry or unhappy, one of my hairs turns white."

The little girl thought about this for a while and said, "Mommy, how come ALL of Grandma's hairs are white?"

ON THE first day of school, the kindergarten teacher said, "If anyone has to go to the bathroom, hold up two fingers." A little voice from the back of the room asked, "How will that help?"

A FOUR-year-old went with his dad to see a litter of kittens. When they returned home, the boy breathlessly informed his mother that there were two boy kittens and two girl kittens.

"How did you know that?" his mother asked.

"Daddy picked them up and looked underneath," he replied. "I think it's printed on the bottom."

The Senility Prayer

GOD GRANT me the senility to forget the people I never liked anyway, the good fortune to run into the ones I do, and the eyesight to tell the difference.

NOW THAT I am older, here's what I have discovered:

1. I started out with nothing, and I still have most of it.
2. My wild oats have turned into prunes and All Bran.
3. I finally got my head together; now my body is falling apart.
4. Funny, I don't remember being absent-minded.
5. All reports are in; life is now officially unfair.
6. If all is not lost, where is it?
7. It is easier to get older than it is to get wiser.
8. Some days you're the dog; some days you're the hydrant.
9. I wish the buck stopped here; I sure could use a few.
10. It's hard to make a comeback when you haven't been anywhere.
11. Only time the world beats a path to your door is when you're in the bathroom.
12. If God wanted me to touch my toes, he would have put them on my knees.
13. When I'm finally holding all the cards, why does everyone decide to play chess?
14. The only difference between a rut and a grave is the depth.

15. These days I spend a lot of time thinking about the hereafter . . . I go somewhere to get something, and then wonder what I'm here after.

A MOTHER was preparing pancakes for her sons Kevin, five, and Ryan, three. The boys began to argue over who would get the first pancake.

Their mother saw the opportunity for a moral lesson, "If Jesus were sitting here, He would say, 'Let my brother have the first pancake. I can wait.'"

Kevin turned to his younger brother and said, "Ryan, you be Jesus."

Father Pettipas is a fan of the cartoon character Dilbert. Dilbert's twenty-five rules of order could easily be condensed into a modern-day Ten Commandments of life and business:

1. Tell me what you need, and I'll tell you how to get along without it.
2. Do not meddle in the affairs of dragons, because you are crunchy and taste good with ketchup.
3. Never argue with an idiot. They drag you down to their level, and then beat you with experience.
4. A pat on the back is only a few centimetres from a kick in the butt.
5. Don't be irreplaceable—if you can't be replaced, you can't be promoted.
6. The more crap you put up with, the more crap you are going to get.
7. You can go anywhere you want if you look serious and carry a clipboard.
8. Eat one live toad the first thing in the morning and nothing worse will happen to you the rest of the day.
9. When you don't know what to do, walk fast and look worried.
10. Don't let yesterday take up too much of today.

Father Gerald A. Dunphy

St. Joseph Parish
Sydney, Nova Scotia

"Humour is such a personal thing," Father Dunphy wrote to me. And he proved it by sending me a few of his personal favourite jokes:

WHEN I was a young priest, I stopped one day to chat with two little girls who lived near the church. They were playing with their little puppy. When I leaned over to be at their level, one of the girls asked what was the white thing around my neck.

"That's my collar," I explained.

She replied, "Does someone take you for a walk every day?"

A CHILD was told by her catechist how to pray. "Just go home, talk to God and listen to what God has to say."

The next week, the child told her catechist. "I did exactly what you told me, but all I could hear was me talking to myself."

AN OLDER couple found a bottle with a magic genie inside. "You may have one wish each," the genie said.

The wife had always wanted to go on a world cruise so she asked for tickets and poof! she had tickets for a cruise around the world.

"I wish I had a wife thirty years younger than me," said the man, and poof! he was ninety years old.

A MAN and his buddy, who had just arrived in town, went to a downtown thrift store to buy some clothes.

The newcomer didn't know what size to ask for so he asked his buddy for advice. "You look to be about a size larger than me," his friend said. "So when I get something you get the next size larger."

Everything worked out fine. The man bought size nine shoes when his buddy got size eight shoes; he got size thirty-six pants when his buddy got size thirty-five; a size sixteen shirt when his friend got size fifteen.

When his friend asked for a hat size six and seven-eighths, the newcomer asked for size nine, ten and eleven.

Father Raphael A. Glofcheski

Winnipeg, Manitoba

Father Glofcheski and I have a lot in common, besides our appreciation of a good, light-hearted story. I am a former air force brat (my father was in the RCAF) and one of our many postings was in the far northern radar base of Moisie, Quebec. Father Glofcheski retired from the armed forces in 1987 and admits to knowing many "air force and army brats" over the years.

He is not assigned to any particular parish in Winnipeg, but has worked in just about all of them. He worked initially, after his return to civilian life, in his home area in the Ottawa Valley. Then he "retired" again to Winnipeg, and says he hasn't stopped working since. He enjoys his replacement work and also his positions as chaplain for the Legion, the Knights of Columbus and the CWL. Each weekend finds him in a different parish, and once a month he drives three hours north to the Lake Manitoba Reserve. He shared this personal story with me, one that still makes him chuckle nearly forty years later:

> IN THE MID-1960s, our Canadian Forces service personnel manned the Pine Tree Line. Most of these northern postings were so remote that families were not permitted to move to the base. However, at Christmastime each soldier was allowed to bring in one family member for a holiday visit.
>
> Also each year, at Christmas and Easter, priests were allocated to go to each of these northern posts to celebrate Mass. At this one particular place in northern Ontario, the following scene unfolded:
>
> The family members and the priest were present and preparing to celebrate Midnight Mass.
>
> As a bit of background, one of the young servicemen had a trained muskrat as a pet. The little critter had grown up to expect a bit of whisky, each day, from the bar. This particular young serviceman had invited his mother to visit the base for the Christmas season.
>
> All was ready. Christmas Eve Mass was being celebrated in the gymnasium. Protestant and Catholics alike were gathered. The priest was about halfway through the service when a noisy ruckus at the back of the gym interrupted the proceedings.
>
> It turned out that the mother of the owner of the muskrat also had a liking for whisky. When she reached into her large purse to get a nip from her flask, her hand met with a warm furry surprise! Apparently, the little muskrat was the first one to get to the bottle. The lady was quite startled and became quite verbal. When both muskrat and mother settled down, the memorable Mass continued.

Father John Appelman, MHM

St. Mark's
Prescott, Ontario

WHILE VISITING the grade two children at school in preparation for their First Holy Communion, I talked to them about the hosts. I said, "The people in the church receive a small host, and the priest takes a big one for himself." I then asked, "Why does the priest have a big one?"

After some deep thinking, one child said, "Because the priest has a big mouth."

Father Michael Machacek

St. Martin de Porres
Scarborough, Ontario

Father Machacek was an engineer before becoming a priest, so he and I traded engineer jokes. The first one is his contribution; the second one's an old engineering joke I passed along to him:

THREE ENGINEERS were in a car. There was an electrical engineer, a chemical engineer, and a computer engineer who worked for Microsoft.

Suddenly, the car's engine went dead and the driver was forced to pull off to the side of the road. The three engineers looked at one another, and wondered what could be wrong.

The electrical engineer suggested they strip down the electronics of the car and try to trace where a fault might have occurred.

The chemical engineer, not knowing much about cars, suggested that maybe the fuel was emulsified and it was getting blocked somewhere.

Then, the Microsoft engineer came up with a suggestion: "If we close all the windows, get out, get back in, then open the windows again, maybe it'll work!"

A PRIEST, a drunkard and an engineer were led to the guillotine. The executioners asked the priest if he wanted to be face up or face down when he met his fate. The priest said he would like to be face up so he would be looking toward heaven when he died.

The blade of the guillotine was raised. It was released, and it came speeding down. Suddenly, it came to a stop, just inches from the priest's neck.

The authorities took this as a divine miracle and they released the priest.

Next, the drunkard was led to the guillotine. He also decided to be face up, hoping that he would be as fortunate as the priest. The blade of the guillotine was raised, then released, and it came speeding down. Again, suddenly, it stopped just inches from his neck. So, they released the drunkard as well.

The engineer was next. He, too, decided to die face up. The blade of the guillotine was slowly raised, when the engineer suddenly said, "Hey, I see what your problem is!"

Father Wallace Metcalf

Regina Mundi Parish
Hamilton, Ontario

Father Metcalf admits that in his thirteen-plus years as a priest, a number of humorous things have happened in church, in the confessional, in the continuing care unit of the local hospital where he ministers, in schools, and in . . . well, humour is just about everywhere. And he has found it, as it has found him. Some of his anecdotes happened very recently, and some "long enough ago that I can laugh at them now."

A LITTLE girl at confession stated that she "accidentally broke her brother's leg."

I went through the long explanation about the fact that accidents are not sins, and that they need not be confessed.

Then she said, "Oh, yes, I lied as well."

"What was your lie?" I had to ask.

"It wasn't an accident" she replied.

I WAS listening to children's first confessions. In one of the schools there was a set of twin boys. After each of them came forward for reconciliation, their mother came up to me and asked: "What did my sons confess?"

Of course, I couldn't tell her, and said so.

"Oh, dear," she answered, "I guess I'll never find out which of them broke the lamp."

Father Ron Coté

Holy Rosary Parish

Burlington, Ontario

Father Coté submitted this true story through Pam Cupido as it was relayed to them by a mother in the parish at the church on Plains Road East in Burlington. How's that for a recycled story?

> FIVE-YEAR-OLD Matthew was being tucked into bed one evening, along with the other children.
>
> As they said their prayers, Matthew expressed concern about his daddy, who was not home at the time. His mother included a prayer for Daddy so that God would protect him from anything bad happening until he got home.
>
> "But God can't help us, Mommy," said Matthew. "I know that from school."
>
> His mother was horrified. "What do you mean, Matthew? Certainly He can!"
>
> "No, He can't," responded Matthew. "Every day we sing, 'O Canada, we stand on God for thee.'"

Father Karl Strickler

White Fathers of Africa

This next story comes by way of Africa, Switzerland and Alberta. Priska Strickler and her family moved from Switzerland to Alberta, near Edmonton, in 1970. When she read an article in The Catholic Register *about my plans to publish* God's Jesters, *she recalled a story that her uncle told her many years ago. Her uncle was "Pater" Karl Strickler, a missionary with the White Fathers of Africa. He spent most of his life on that continent, and his last and longest stay was in Malawi. Father Strickler died in 1995 at the age of seventy-two. His niece thinks he would be pleased to have this true anecdote repeated:*

> DURING MOST of his career, Father Karl lived in areas where white people were rarely seen. One Sunday, a white Englishwoman appeared in the congregation. When the collection basket was passed around, she dropped a substantial amount of money in the basket.
>
> Since the local people had only pennies to spare, it was quite evident where the lion's share came from that day. My uncle

always greeted the churchgoers as they left. Although his command of the English language was very limited, he thanked the Englishwoman for her generous "droppings."

Only later did he realize, to his horror, what he had said!

Father Romeo Major

Canadian Martyrs Parish

Cornwall, Ontario

In honour of Pope John Paul II's visit to Toronto for World Youth Day in July 2002, Father Romeo Major thought it would be apropos to submit a "pope joke" . . . along with several others:

JOHN PAUL II once came to Canada incognito. While in Toronto he asked his chauffeur if he could drive for a while. The chauffeur considered this an unusual request, but what could he say? So, they traded places. The pope climbed behind the steering wheel and his chauffeur sat in the back of the stretch limousine.

Naturally, the pope was unfamiliar with Toronto streets, and at one point he drove in the wrong direction on a one-way street.

A police officer stopped the vehicle. When he approached the car, he was understandably shocked. He excused himself and returned to his police car.

He called his supervisor and reported, "I just stopped someone going the wrong way on a one-way street. I don't know the person sitting in the back, but he's some kind of a big celebrity. Should I give him a ticket?"

"Is it the premier?" the supervisor asked.

"No, bigger."

"The prime minister?"

"No, it's someone more important than that. I have no idea who it is but he has the pope as his chauffeur."

JOHN WAS in church saying the Rosary. When he heard someone call his name he looked around, but the church was empty.

Soon, he heard his name being called again.

He looked all around. Not a soul in view. He kept on praying the Rosary. Again, he heard his name. So, he called out, "Who are you?"

The voice answered, "It's me, Jesus."

John said, "Be quiet. Can't you see I'm talking to your mother?"

A WOMAN was talking to her husband after Mass. "The priest delivered a poor homily . . . no theme, no sense, no end."

Her husband agreed, and added that the choir was awful, ". . . no harmony, plenty of discord and screeching."

Their son said, "I thought you got a pretty good show for your quarter."

A COUPLE died just before their marriage. When they met St. Peter at the Gates of Heaven, they asked if they could get married in heaven.

He said he would look into it.

They waited for a month without a response from St. Peter. Meanwhile, they were wondering if they could ever get a divorce if they wanted, since being in heaven was for eternity.

Two months after their initial request, St. Peter told them that their union could indeed be blessed in heaven.

When they inquired about the possibility of a divorce sometime in the future, St. Peter became angry. "It took me two months to find a priest. Now you want me to look for a lawyer?"

A MAN kept his hat on before Mass started one Sunday morning. The usher approached him and asked him to remove his hat.

The man refused.

The Grand Knight of the Knights of Columbus spoke to him about taking his hat off.

No way.

The Regent of the Daughters of Isabella came forward to advise him how inappropriate it was to wear a hat in church.

No success.

Finally, the pastor approached him for the same reason. The man replied, "I've been coming to this church for the past two months and nobody has spoken to me. This morning, because of my hat, four people have talked to me."

A NEW priest, on his first Sunday in the new parish, delivered a beautiful homily. Many parishioners congratulated him.

The following Sunday, he delivered the same sermon.

Some people thought he just didn't have time to prepare a new sermon.

On the third Sunday, he gave the same homily.

The people were becoming very concerned, so the president of the Parish Council told him, "You've been here for three Sundays and you have given the same homily each Sunday. You made no changes."

The priest replied, "I agree! I delivered the same sermon three times in a row and it's true that nothing has changed in the parish."

A YOUNG lad wanted a bicycle so he prayed to Jesus to get him a bike.

Christmas came, and he did not receive a bike.

He kept on praying.

His birthday came. No bike.

So, he took a statue of the Blessed Virgin, wrapped her in a towel and put it in a drawer. Then, kneeling to pray, he said to the Lord, "If you want your mother back, get me a bike."

Father Bill Penney

Holy Name of Mary Parish

Almonte, Ontario

Native Newfoundlander (from St. John's) Father Penney publishes a "Morning Smile" in his Sunday Bulletin each week. Some of his parishioners have told him the first thing they do before leaving the church parking lot after Mass is to read the joke of the week. Father Penney said he would be "delighted" to have some of his favourites published in God's Jesters:

ON A cold, wintry Sunday in January, only the priest and one farmer arrived at the village church. The pastor said, "Well I guess we won't have Mass today." The farmer replied, "Heck, if even only one cow shows up at feeding time, I still feed it."

The priest was impressed with the farmer's forthright manner, so he proceeded with the Mass and delivered a forty-five-minute sermon. When he was finished, the farmer said, "But I wouldn't give it the whole load."

A CERTAIN janitor had the apostolic practice of ringing the church bells loud and long, especially on Sunday mornings.

When some of the neighbouring parishioners complained, he growled, "If they're not coming to church, they're not going to sleep, either."

THE TOWN drunk was staggering home with a pint of booze in his back pocket when he slipped and fell heavily. As he struggled to his feet he felt something wet running down his leg. "Please, God," he implored. "Let that be blood."

TWO INEBRIATED men wandered into a wake. They were so drunk they couldn't even find the corpse.

For ten minutes they stood solemnly in front of a grand piano. Finally, one nudged the other and said, "Do you recognize him?"

The other replied, "No, but he sure had a fine set of teeth."

AFTER A long sermon, the priest announced that he wished to meet with the church board at the end of the Mass.

The first man to arrive and greet the priest was a total stranger. "You misunderstood my announcement," explained the priest. "This is a meeting of the board."

"I know," replied the man. "If there is anyone here more bored than I am, then I'd like to meet him."

THREE MEN who were sitting behind a couple of nuns at an NFL football game decided to badger the nuns in an effort to get them to move.

In a very loud voice, the first guy said, "I think I'm going to move to Utah—there are only about a hundred Catholics living there."

The second guy spoke up and said, "I want to go to Montana. There are even fewer Catholics living there."

The third guy spoke up and said, "I want to go to Idaho—there are only a few dozen Catholics there."

One of the nuns turned around, looked at the men, and calmly said, "Why don't you go to hell? There aren't any Catholics there."

A STUDENT was talking about whales to her agnostic teacher. The teacher said it was impossible for a whale to swallow a human because, even though it is a very large animal, its throat is very small.

The student stated that Jonah was swallowed by a whale.

Irritated, the teacher repeated that a whale could not swallow a human; it is physically impossible.

The student said, "When I get to heaven I will ask Jonah."

The teacher asked, "What if Jonah went to hell?"

The student replied, "Then you ask him."

A DOCTOR kneeled down and said, "I'd like to pray to St. Luke, patron saint of doctors and surgeons."

A reply came from above, "Sorry, you'll have to make an appointment."

EVE CALLED out from the Garden of Eden, "Lord, I have a problem."

The Lord said, "What's the matter, Eve?"

She replied, "I know you created me and this beautiful garden. But I'm lonely and I'm sick of eating apples."

"Well, in that case," God replied, "I'll create a man for you."

"What's a man?"

"He's a flawed creature with aggressive tendencies, an enormous ego and an inability to listen. But he's big and fast and muscular. He's good at fighting and kicking a ball and hunting animals. And, at times, he can be tender and loving."

"Sounds great!" Eve replied.

"There's one condition, though," added the Lord. "For this to work, you'll have to let him believe that I made him first."

AN ELDERLY gentleman was on his deathbed, so he called his friend and said, "Bill, I want you to promise me that when I die, you will have my remains cremated."

His friend asked, "And what do you want me to do with your ashes?"

The man replied, "Just put them in an envelope and mail them to the tax department in Ottawa. Write on the envelope, 'Now, you have everything.'"

A WOMAN'S husband had been slipping in and out of a coma for several months, yet she stayed by his bedside every single day.

One day, when he came to, he motioned for her to come nearer. As she sat by him, he whispered, eyes full of tears. "You have been with me through all the bad times. When I got fired, you were there to support me. When my business failed, you were there for me. When I got shot, you were by my side. When we lost our home to fire, you stayed right beside me. When my health started to fail, you were still by my side. You know what?"

"What, dear," she gently asked.

"I think you're bad luck!"

Church Bulletin Bloopers:

- There will be a potluck supper with prayer and medication to follow.
- We will re-enact the Last Supper and journey to the Garden of Gethsemane on Holy Thursday, March 29 at 7 p.m. We will strip the altar and sanctuary of all colour and symbol. Together, we will leave the church bare and in silence.
- As the maintenance of the cemetery is becoming increasingly costly, it would be appreciated if those who are willing would clip the grass around their own graves.

THE PRIEST'S opening prayer began, "O God, give us clean hearts, give us pure hearts, give us sweet hearts . . ." and three ladies in the choir added, "Amen!"

MONEY:

It can buy a house, but not a home.

It can buy a bed, but not sleep.

It can buy a clock, but not time.

It can buy you a book, but not knowledge.

It can buy you a position, but not respect.

It can buy you medicine, but not health.

It can buy you sex, but not love.

So, you see, money isn't everything, and it often causes pain and suffering. I tell you this because I am your friend, and as your friend I want to take away all your pain. So, please give me all your money and I will suffer for you.

Father Leo J. Trainor

Stella Maris Parish,
North Rustico, P.E.I.

On June 4, 2002, I spent part of an afternoon chatting with Father Trainor in his living room, trading quips and some stories about his "colleagues of the collar." The man is the spitting image of Minnesota governor and former professional wrestler Jesse Ventura. More than one Islander had insisted that I meet Father Trainor, including Island-born John Watson, a professional photographer in Vancouver, and my Aunt Kal McCloskey who was visited by Father Trainor when she was recovering from heart surgery. "He's a real corker," she said.

Ranger, a huge, rangy dog that used to join Father Trainor on the altar during church services, sat with us on this June afternoon. Some parishioners were upset to see a dog at the altar, and wrote a letter to the bishop, who in turn wrote to Father Trainor. "As a result," said Father Trainor, "Ranger is the only dog in Canada that's banned from church by the bishop." He then led me across the parking lot and into the entrance of the church. There, on the left wall, is a large, colour photograph of Father Leo Trainor and his faithful dog, Ranger. Seeing the picture reminded me of this well-worn story:

A FARMER named Muldoon lived alone in the Irish countryside with a pet dog he doted on. The dog finally died and Muldoon went to the parish priest, saying, "Father, the dog is dead. Could you possibly be saying a Mass for the poor creature?"

Father Patrick said to the farmer, "No, we can't have services for an animal in the church, but I'll tell you what, there's a new denomination down the road, and no telling what they believe in, but maybe they'll do something for the animal."

Muldoon said, "I'll go right now. By the way, do you think $10,000 is enough to donate for the service?"

Father Patrick replied, "Why didn't you tell me the dog was Catholic?"

I met Father Trainor the day after he returned home from Halifax, Nova Scotia, where he had been attending a conference. He reached into his yet-unpacked briefcase and began reading some of the jokes and humour stories that he had told at the conference. Here's one of them:

A MAN who'd had a few drinks was in the room when his wife was giving birth. The doctor announced that it was a boy. The man raised his glass in celebration.

"Wait a second," said the doctor. "Here comes another. It's twins!"

A minute later the doctor cried out, "No, wait. It's triplets." Then, in astonishment, he yelled, "Quads!"

The shaken doctor asked the husband to hold the light closer so he could see if there were any more babies in there.

The husband took another drink and said, "No sir! I think it's the light that's attracting them."

Father John Asadoorian

(When he was Associate Pastor, St. Mary Immaculate)
Richmond Hill, Ontario

In the 1980s, I wrote a story for a corporate magazine about Massis Asadoorian, who had built a Spezio Tuholer airplane in the driveway of his Oshawa home. Massis, who is now deceased, took me for the ride of my life over the lakes and fields of Ontario's beautiful Kawartha district. When I met his son, Father John, many years later, I told the young priest that I kept thinking of one hymn over and over during the flight with his dad. It was, "Nearer My God To Thee"!

Father John spent some time assisting at our parish church in Richmond Hill in the late 1990s. He got a good response when he related this joke from the altar one Sunday morning:

A PRIEST decided to sell his horse. A prospective buyer was impressed with the animal, but the priest said, "I must warn you—he responds only to 'church talk.' 'Go' is 'Praise the Lord' and 'stop' is 'Hallelujah.'"

"I've worked with horses all my life," said the buyer, "I've never heard of anything like this."

However, he mounted the horse, and said, skeptically, "Praise the Lord."

The horse began to trot.

He repeated, "Praise the Lord," and the horse started to gallop.

Suddenly, the buyer saw a steep cliff dead ahead. Frantic, he yelled, "Hallelujah," and they came to a stop at the edge of the cliff.

Wiping sweat from his brow, the buyer sighed, "Praise the Lord!"

Father Hervé Sauvé

La Transfiguration
Cochrane, Ontario

Father Sauvé likes to treat his 3,000 parishioners in the northern community of Cochrane to a bit of humour from time to time. "I like using jokes and anecdotes during the Sunday celebrations to show people that church doesn't always have to be serious," he wrote to me. Here are two of his pet anecdotes:

> A FEW years ago, I was visiting the grade school in my parish with our bishop (Bishop Vallée) in the diocese of Hearst. We visited several classes and we finally got to the grade five class. They all knew who I was, but the person who was with me intrigued them. I told them he was my boss. They were all surprised, and I further told them that he was my bishop and his name was Bishop Vallée.
>
> One of the little girls raised her hand and told me that she, too, had a "big ship."

> WHILE MAKING my parish visits one day, the young boy of the family I was visiting saw me coming to their house. He went to his mother and said, "Mom, God is coming."
>
> The mother replied, "What?"
>
> He repeated, "God is here, and he's coming to our house, except that today he is wearing a housecoat."

Father Dennis J. Noon

St. Joseph's Parish
Guelph, Ontario

The 16,000 parishioners at St. Joseph's, on Paisley Road in Guelph, have heard Father Dennis Noon say this before: "Priests should write down their many stories and experiences."

I gave him the opportunity to write down a few of his favourite stories and (besides being blessed with a great first name!) Father Dennis proved he has a great sense of humour by relating the following true *anecdotes:*

> ON THE first Sunday of Advent, as I proceeded down the aisle in my new purple vestments, a four-year-old boy shouted out, "Look, Mom, here comes Barney!"

> UPON MY ordination, my five-year-old nephew, David, asked me why everyone was coming up to me and calling me "Father." He said, "You are not a dad like my father, you are one of them fake fathers."

> WHEN I was an associate, my pastor was known for being rather dramatic in his reading of the scriptures. One Sunday, he was readi ng the Gospel for the Mass of the Epiphany when he said, "And they came, bringing gifts of gold, Frankenstein and myrrh."

Father Louis McCloskey

St. Theresa's Roman Catholic Church
West St. Paul, Manitoba

If I thought Father Dennis Noon was blessed with a great first name, I'd say that Father Louis McCloskey was doubly blessed with his surname! In fact, the Winnipeg area priest was born and raised in the land of my birth (P.E.I.). His mother was Marie Cahill (I have an aunt in Charlottetown by the same name), and Father McCloskey knows lots of my living and late relatives from east to west on the Island.

We exchanged some family history: his father's grandparents, James and Mary (Murray) McCloskey were married in Enniskillen Fermanagh, Ireland, and immigrated from Emyvale County Monaghan to Emyvale, P.E.I. around 1850. That could be more information than you need to know, but here's a delightful personal anecdote from (who knows?) my distant relative?

> A COUPLE of days after Christmas, I received a phone call asking why there was no Christmas Midnight Mass.
>
> I replied that we'd had Mass earlier, at ten p.m. on Christmas Eve, and I had announced the change in plenty of time in the bulletins and at all the Sunday Masses during Advent.
>
> The caller defensively replied, "Well, how would we know that? We don't go to Mass on Sundays."

Father F. J. Power, S. J.

Apostleship of Prayer
Editor, *Canadian Messenger of the Sacred Heart*
Toronto, Ontario

Father Power has published several of my articles in his monthly Catholic magazine, Canadian Messenger. *When I asked him if he had any jokes for* God's Jesters, *he said he had a couple of favourites. As with most editors, his stories are short, concise and to the point. Here's one:*

A MAN goes to confession and confesses that he is responsible for blowing up several railway cars.

The priest gave him the penance: "Do the stations."

Father Elias Chachati

Administrator, St. Ann Parish

Penetanguishene, Ontario

When I contacted Father Chachati, he had been assigned to St. Ann Parish following the death of Msgr. Leonard P. O'Malley C.H.H., who passed away October 18, 2001. Father Chachati had a few jokes that he said might be suitable for publication in God's Jesters. *We both agreed that Msgr. O'Malley might be smiling in heaven.*

DOCTOR TO patient: "I can't find the cause of your illness. It's probably due to drinking." Patient: "I understand. I'll come back when you're sober."

PATIENT TO doctor: "Doctor, I think I know what's wrong with me." Doctor: "I do, too. I've been watching the same television program."

A WOMAN picked up the phone, dialled 9–1–1 and cried out in a panicky voice, "Operator! Operator!"

"One moment, please!"

"But this is an emergency! My husband has a 130-degree temperature!"

"Okay, I'll connect you with the fire department."

Father Michael Mahoney

Sacred Heart Parish

Sioux Lookout, Ontario

Father Mahoney found this cute story in the desk of a former pastor:

A GROUP of children in Hallowe'en costumes gathered outside Father Murphy's house. They knocked on the door and waited, but nothing happened.

Then, one little boy shouted, "We know you're in there, Father, so turn on the light and come out with your hands full!"

Father Viateur (Vic) Laurin

Assomption de Notre-Dame Church
Oshawa, Ontario

When I asked Father Laurin if he would like to contribute to my book, he said: "Yes, I am ready to do almost anything—even humiliate myself—just to see my name in print!" Father Laurin "swears" the following conversation took place a few years ago between himself and the female clerk working at the courtesy desk at the local A&P store:

> I APPROACHED the lady at the grocery store's service desk and said, "I would like $700 worth of gift coupons."
>
> "My, my! I know most men don't like Christmas shopping, but this is the ultimate!" she joked.
>
> "Oh, it's not for me personally, it's for my church," I said. "We've decided to give gift certificates to needy families this year, instead of the usual Christmas baskets."
>
> "That's a good idea!" she replied. "That way, people can buy what they really want. I'll have them ready by two o'clock this afternoon. Oh, by the way, in what denominations?"
>
> "Catholic, Protestant, or any other," I said proudly. "We help everybody!"

Father Brendan J. McCarthy

Parish of Saint Joseph and Saint Patrick
Port Union, Newfoundland & Labrador

Father Brendan McCarthy is an Irishman and a Newfoundlander who ministers to the 1,000 Roman Catholics in Port Union and the missions of Bonavista and Trinity. As a Newfie from Belfast, you can be sure he has a few tales to tell. The first one concerns his first name. "I was named after the Irish Saint who was a navigator, and who probably discovered Newfoundland before the Vikings," he told me.

He also mentioned that he was working on a book himself, one that will contain a lot of poetry. He added that many of his stories are based on the lessons to be learned from the antics of the Peanuts Gang made famous by the late cartoonist Charles Schulz.

The following is a personal story that Father McCarthy says happened to him "in the days of yore."

I WAS ordained a priest in 1952 when Latin was still the language of Holy Mother Church. I was, at that time, a member of a religious order, and apart from teaching theology, my principal work was hearing confessions.

My brother and his wife had their second child, a boy, just as I was sent by my order to America. Before I left, I agreed to baptize the new arrival in the family. However, the pastor in their parish used a ritual that was printed in an old English script. I had to rely on my memory for most of the ceremony.

Following the baptism, we were driving home with my brother, my mother, the infant's godmother, and me in the back. Suddenly, I had a horrible thought, and I asked my brother, "Can you remember whether I said, '*Ego te baptizo*,' or '*Ego te absolvo?*'" His Latin was somewhat rusty and he confessed he didn't know.

For almost two years after I arrived in America I was tortured by the notion of what might happen should my nephew ultimately want to be a priest . . . no valid ordination, Masses that weren't Masses, absolutions that were not valid. Finally, a solution was offered to me. A Redemptorist friend of mine had returned to Ireland after a spell on the missions. He was stationed in Belfast, my native city. I wrote to him and explained my "problem." He replied quickly: If my brother were to bring the young fellow to the monastery, Father would give him conditional Baptism.

On the appointed day, off went my brother with his "doubtful" Christian son.

When they returned home, my sister-in-law asked the young fellow, "Where were you?"

He answered, "Mummy, me see Father Creagh."

My sister-in-law asked, "What did he do?"

The youngster replied, "Mummy, he shampooed my hair."

Father A. T. Harrington

St. Alphonsus' Church
Chapeau, Quebec

TWO MICE lived in the church. One was very thin and nervous; the other was fat and quite calm. One day they met. The fat one said, "Where do you live?" The skinny mouse said, "I live in the pulpit where the priest talks loud, shouts and stamps his feet. I can't stand it. Where do you live?"

The fat mouse yawned and said, "Oh, I live in the Poor Box. I never hear a sound."

THE BISHOP was confirming a group of children and he asked a little boy, "What is marriage?"

The little boy answered, "It's a place where some souls suffer for a time before they go to heaven."

Amidst peals of laughter, the bishop replied, "More truth than fiction."

Father Eugene B. Morris

Sacred Heart Parish

Badger, Newfoundland & Labrador

Father Morris cares for two parishes (the other one is St. Theresa's in Buchans), and three missions on Pilley's Island and St. Patrick's. He said he was happy to hear about God's Jesters *"because we don't use God's gift of humour as much as we should." Father Morris certainly puts his sense of humour to good use, as you will see:*

A PRIEST was stopped on the highway for speeding. As the police officer began to write out a speeding ticket, the priest pleaded with him, saying, "Please don't fine me. I am just a poor preacher."

The police officer replied, "I know. I heard you last Sunday."

A DEAF woman, who spoke very loudly in the confessional, was told by the priest to write down her sins and pass them to him in the confessional.

At her next confession she passed the priest a list, which read, "One lb. of tea, six oranges, ten lbs. of potatoes and a loaf of bread."

When the priest read her list aloud, the woman moaned, "Oh my God! I left all my sins at the grocery store!"

A YOUNG priest told his congregation that he always fasted before preaching. "I always preach better if I do not eat," he said, with a certain amount of pride.

After Mass, as the young priest was bidding farewell to the departing parishioners, one lady remarked to him, "You might as well have ate, Father."

A PRIEST was walking past a graveyard when he noticed a man kneeling by a grave in apparent uncontrolled grief. The man was beating the grave with his fists and sobbing, "Why did you have to die? Why did you have to die?"

Being a compassionate person, the priest approached the distraught man who continued to cry out, "Why, oh why, did you die?"

"This must have been someone who was very dear to you," said the man of God. "Was it a close friend or a family member?"

"No," sighed the man. "It was my wife's first husband."

A PREACHER urged his people to grow in holiness. "You have to stop sinning—really stop—because it's not good enough just to slow down."

Some time later he was pulled over by a police officer for not coming to a complete stop at an intersection. "Well, I almost stopped," said the preacher. "I slowed down. What's the difference?"

The police officer took out his nightstick and began to hit the preacher with it. As he kept hitting him, the officer said, "Do you want me to stop or just slow down?"

Father Hugh Gibson

St. Joseph Church

Grimsby, Ontario

Tracy Piggott is the secretary at St. Joseph's in Grimsby, and everyone knows the church secretary rules the roost, so it was Tracy who wrested some funny stories from the pastor and assistant pastor.

TWO BOYS, aged eight and ten, were terribly mischievous, so much so that whenever some mischief occurred at school or in the neighbourhood, the boys' parents would assume—often correctly—that their two sons were involved.

When all of their disciplinary efforts had failed, the parents were at their wits' end. Then the mother heard that the new priest in town had a history of success in dealing with children who get into trouble. She contacted him and he agreed to speak to the boys—one at a time.

When the eight-year-old walked in, the priest frowned at him, told him to sit down, and began his lecture by asking, in a stern voice, "Where is God?"

There was no answer.

Again, the priest repeated the question in an even sterner tone, "Where is God?"

Again, no answer.

The priest raised his voice even louder, shook his finger in the boy's face and asked a third time, "Where is God?"

The frightened youngster bolted out of the room and ran to where his older brother was waiting.

"What happened?" asked the brother.

"We're in big trouble this time," came the reply. "God is missing and they think we did it!"

Father Edward Jankowski

(Lt. Col. Ret'd, Assisting Pastor)
St. Joseph Church
Grimsby, Ontario

IN THE late 1950s, I was a curate in a parish not far from my family home. One Easter Monday, I decided to visit my family. When I told my pastor of my plan, he asked if I would mind taking one of the nuns to visit with her parents, who lived in a town that I would pass on my way. I readily agreed.

The nun was dressed in her black habit, and when we arrived at her parents' home, her mother immediately phoned her daughter-in-law to inform her of Sister's visit. The young mother arrived shortly, with her pre-school daughter in tow. During the course of the visit, the little girl whispered something into her mother's ear.

The mother then asked the child, "Aren't you going to tell Sister your secret?"

The little girl glanced at Sister and exclaimed, "You have no ears!"

Father Harry W. Rasmussen, SDB

Our Lady of Good Counsel Parish
Surrey, British Columbia

On March 17, 2002, I was doing some "research" for God's Jesters *in B.C. Being a good Irish Catholic, I attended Mass on St. Patrick's Day. My brother, Wayne, who teaches at Our Lady of Sorrows in Vancouver, took me to his family's church, St. Michael, on Holmes Street in Burnaby. The church is known for its magnificent backdrop view (as you face the altar) of majestic trees and mountains. Wayne introduced me to his pastor, Msgr. Bernard A. Rossi, and we had a pleasant conversation after Mass. When I mentioned to him that I was collecting the favourite jokes of Canadian priests, he couldn't think of any "off the cuff," but he assured me that the priests in the area were not without a sense of humour and that I would surely be successful in my quest from some of the neighbouring clergy.*

He was right. Here are four favourites from Father Harry Rasmussen who resides and tends to his flock in the community right next door to Burnaby:

> YEARS AGO, an old lady down south had no money to buy food. But with complete trust in God, she got down on her knees and prayed aloud, "Dear Lord, please send me a side of bacon and a sack of cornmeal."
>
> Over and over again the old lady repeated the same plea in a loud voice.
>
> One of the town's most detestable characters overheard her supplication one day and decided to play a trick on the old woman. He hurried to the nearest store and bought a side of bacon and a sack of cornmeal. When he returned to the woman's ramshackle cabin, he dropped the food down the chimney. It landed right in front of the hungry woman as she knelt in prayer.
>
> She got to her feet and exclaimed in jubilation, "O Lord, you've answered my prayer!" Then she went all around the neighbourhood to tell everyone the good news.
>
> This was too much for the scoundrel. He ridiculed her before the whole town by telling how he, himself, had dropped the food down the chimney.
>
> The old woman quickly replied, "Well, the devil may have brought it, but it was the Lord who sent it!"

> EARLY ONE Sunday morning an Anglican woman hurried into her son's bedroom and raised her voice at the sleeping bundle. "It's Sunday. Time to get up and go to church!"
>
> The son mumbled from under the covers, "I don't want to go."
>
> "What do you mean, 'I don't want to go'?" shouted the mother. "That's silly. Now get up, get dressed and go to church!"
>
> "No, I don't want to go and I'll give you two reasons why not," he said, now wide-awake. He sat up in bed and continued, "First, I don't like the people who go to that church and second, they don't like me."

The mother replied, "That's just plain nonsense. You've got to go to church and I'll give you two reasons why you have to go. First, you're fifty-one years old, and, second, you're the pastor!"

A LAZY frog lived in a forest in New Jersey. One late autumn day, he persuaded two geese to fly him down to Florida for the winter. He tied the end of a long cord to each of the geese and he held the centre of the cord in his mouth, and off they went.

The journey was going well until a boy on the ground noticed the strange sight passing by overhead. "Hey, look at that!" shouted the boy. "That's fantastic! Whose idea was that, I wonder?"

The frog wanted to get all the credit for being so clever, so he opened his mouth and shouted, "Mine!"

Father Frank J. Franz

Holy Family/Notre Dame Roman Catholic Parish
Port Alberni, British Columbia

A LOST travelling salesman stopped at a farmyard for directions. After thanking the farmer for his help, on his way out he noticed in the field a pig with a wooden leg. He thought it strange but drove on. The thought of the pig with the wooden leg haunted him in the weeks to come. No matter how he tried he couldn't get the image out of his mind. "A pig with a wooden leg!"

About a month later he again found himself in the vicinity of the farm where months earlier he had stopped to ask directions. "I must stop and ask why that pig has a wooden leg," he thought to himself. As he drove into the farmyard he saw the pig again, this time with two wooden legs. Scratching his head, he said to the farmer, "Last time I was here that pig had one wooden leg. Now it has two wooden legs. I must know why!"

"Simple," replied the farmer. "That pig wins first prize at every fair in the area. Good pig like that, you don't eat all at once!"

A MOSTLY bald man, with three hairs on his head—one on the left side, one on the right and one straight up in the middle—went to the barbershop. He flopped into the chair and told the barber he wanted a trim.

The barber took the scissors, went snip-snip-snip, announced to the man the haircut was over and showed him the results in the mirror. The man then asked the barber to part his hair on the left.

The barber tried to comb the single hair down but the comb yanked the hair out. "That's okay," the man said. "Comb my hair to the right." The barber tried to comb the single hair to the right but the comb yanked out that hair. The customer was exasperated. He said to the barber, "Never mind! Just leave it messy!"

Father Andrew Cyruk

Notre Dame Parish

North Battleford, Saskatchewan

On January 30, 2002, the fax machine rang in my home office and out came ten pages of jokes. "Here are a 'few' jokes," wrote Father Cyruk. "I hope you can use some for your book. Let me know if you need more."

I WAS visiting one of the families in our parish and the mother was becoming very upset with her teen-age son at the supper table. She said, "Son, I wish you would stop reaching for things. Don't you have a tongue?"

The son replied, "Yeah, but my arm is longer!"

A MAN who had dated the same woman for twenty years finally married her.

A friend said to him, "Joe, why didn't you marry that splendid woman long before now? Why did you wait all these years?"

"I waited until she'd talked herself out. I wanted a quiet married life!"

AFTER WATCHING a priest toss coins with a parishioner to see who would pay for a restaurant meal, a friend asked, "Father, isn't that gambling?"

"Not at all," the priest replied. "It's simply a scientific method of determining just who is going to commit an act of charity."

A NEWLY WED couple was visiting a friend when they were asked, "How do you like your new house? Are you meeting expenses?"

"Meeting expenses is no problem! Every time we turn around—there they are!"

A TWELVE-YEAR-OLD boy was asked why he thinks he has the best mother in the world.

He announced, "She stays on speaking terms with God, and on spanking terms with me!"

THE RECTOR of a seminary addressed a group of would-be priests with the following announcement: "All seminarians who like music please come to my office."

Ten students showed up.

He looked them over and said, "Now, then—get busy and carry that piano up to the top floor."

A FAMILY doctor had just left a home after making a rare house call.

The family's four-year-old daughter asked, "Mommy, who was that man?"

"He brought you into this world."

The daughter replied, "That was GOD?"

THE FUSSY priest was not happy with the cook who substituted for the housekeeper on her vacation.

He complained to a member of the congregation. "She treats me like a Greek god! She places a burnt offering before me at every meal!"

A PRIEST was visiting a parishioner who had an unusually large collection of books. He noticed that the books were piled high and spread around the room in great disorder.

He remarked, "Why don't you get some bookcases?"

The book collector had a ready explanation, "Well, Father, it's not hard to borrow books, but it's very hard to borrow bookcases!"

A WOMAN walked up to a little old man rocking in a chair on his porch.

"I couldn't help noticing how happy you look," she said. "What's your secret for a long, happy life?"

"I smoke three packs of cigarettes a day," he said. "I also drink a case of whisky a week, eat fatty foods, and I never exercise!"

"That's amazing," the woman said. "How old are you?"

"Twenty-six."

MR. SMITH was brought to Mercy Catholic Hospital and quickly taken to the operating room for coronary surgery. The operation went well. When the man regained consciousness, a Sister of Mercy, who was waiting by his bed, was comforting him.

"Mr. Smith, you're going to be just fine," said the nun. "However, we do need to know how you intend to pay for your stay here. Are you covered by insurance?"

"No, I'm not," the man whispered.

"Then, can you pay in cash?" asked the nun.

"I'm afraid I cannot, Sister."

The nun was persistent. "Well, do you have any close relatives?"

"Just my sister in New Mexico," he said. "But she is a humble and single nun."

"Oh, I must correct you, Mr. Smith. Nuns are not single. They are married to God."

"Wonderful," said Mr. Smith. "In that case, please send the bill to my brother-in-law."

A MOTHER was teaching her three-year-old the Lord's Prayer. For several evenings at bedtime, the child repeated it after the mother. Then, one night the child was ready to solo. The mother listened with pride to the carefully enunciated words, right up to the end. "And lead us not into temptation, but deliver us some e-mail."

Father Obioma Anyanwu C.S. Sp.

Our Lady of the Annunciation Parish

Hull, Quebec

Father Obioma is a Nigerian whose first name means "Good heart." ("Whether I live up to that meaning is an open-ended discussion," he joked to me.) His surname means "sun" ("that lightens everyone's way").

A member of the religious order Spiritans (Congregation of the Holy Ghost), Father Obioma told me that the flourishing church in eastern Nigeria, where he is from, was started by the Irish priests (he was baptized by a Father Boucley), so he believes there is a little bit o' the Irish humour in him.

A MARRIED couple had more than a few shortcomings between them, and they never gave much credit to each other.

The man felt that his wife had no manners and was anything but kind. The woman saw her husband as a drunkard and good for nothing.

On one occasion, on the night of Hallowe'en, the man was in his usual drunken stupor when his wife decided to frighten him by dressing in a bright red Hallowe'en costume, with horns and a pointed tail. She hid in some bushes near their home and waited for her husband to approach.

When she saw him stagger up the sidewalk, she leaped from her hiding place, making strange noises.

The startled husband asked, "Who the (bleep) are you?"

She replied, "I am the devil!"

The man said, "Then come, let's go to my house. I live with your sister."

CHAPTER FOUR

"Humour is a divine quality, and God has the greatest sense of humour of all. He must have, otherwise he wouldn't have made so many politicians."

Martin Luther King

Father John Kuilboer

Sacred Heart Parish

Langton, Ontario

Worshippers at Sacred Heart in Langton, south of Tillsonburg, Ontario, are treated to a smile every Sunday when they open their Sunday Bulletin. *Father John admitted to me that some of the one-liners are good and some are not so great, but he's pretty sure "for most people, that's all they read out of the thing."*

He said it was "wonderful to hear" that I was publishing this book. He contributed so many good ones that he's been collecting over the years, I felt I'd better devote an entire chapter to him before he "scoops" me with his own book of pastoral jokes. These are but a sample of the ones he sent to me:

A BISHOP went to an unfamiliar church to celebrate the Eucharist. There was a microphone on the altar. At the Entrance Antiphone, he greeted the worshippers, "The Lord be with you." But, being uncertain whether the mike was switched on, he tapped it gently with no result. So, leaning very close to it, he said in a loud whisper, which echoed around the church, "There's something wrong with this microphone."

The well-trained and responsive congregation replied at once, "And also with you."

A PRIEST asked a little boy if he said his prayers every night. "Yes, sir," the boy replied.

"And do you always say them in the morning, too?" the pastor asked.

"No, sir," the boy replied. "I'm not scared in the daytime."

FOUR BISHOPS were on a plane. During the flight, the pilot announced the loss of one of the plane's engines. "No cause to worry," the pilot announced. "We have three good engines working."

An elderly woman asked a stewardess, "Are you sure there is no danger?"

The stewardess replied, "No danger, ma'am. Besides, we have four bishops on board."

The elderly woman replied, "I would rather have four engines and three bishops than three engines and four bishops."

TWO SAILORS were adrift on a raft in the ocean. They had just about given up hope of rescue. One began to pray, "O Lord, I've led a worthless life and neglected my children and been unkind to my wife, but if you'll save me, I promise I . . ."

"Hold it!" the other shouted, "I think I see land!"

A PRIEST was engaged in a conversation with a worldly unbeliever. "I never go to church, Father," the man said. "There are too many hypocrites there."

"Oh, don't let that keep you away," smiled the priest. "There's always room for one more."

WHEN A priest asked the class, "Why was Jesus born in Bethlehem?" a boy raised his hand and replied, "Because his mother was there."

A MAN went to the track and saw a priest bless a horse before a race. The man quickly went to the ticket window and placed a bet. The horse won. He watched the priest carefully for the next four races, and continued to win until he had quite a small fortune. He decided to bet it all on one last race.

Before the horse crossed the finish line however, it dropped dead. The man rushed up to the priest, confronted him with what he had seen and demanded an explanation.

The priest just shook his head in sadness and said, "That's one of the problems with you unbelievers. You don't know the difference between a blessing and the last rites."

THE ANGLICAN minister had been summoned to the bedside of a Catholic woman who was quite ill. As he went up the walk, he met the teenage daughter of the woman and said to her, "I'm very glad your mother remembered me in her illness. Is your priest out of town?"

"No," answered the girl. "He's at home, but we thought it might be something contagious, and we didn't want to expose him to it."

A PRIEST was giving the children a message during a school Mass. On this particular day, he was using squirrels for an object lesson on industry and preparation. He started out by saying, "I'm going to describe something, and I want you to raise your hand when you know what it is."

The children nodded eagerly.

"This thing lives in trees [pause] and eats nuts [pause] . . ."

No hands went up.

"And it is brown [pause] and has a long bushy tail [pause] . . ."

The children looked at each other, but still no hands rose.

"And it jumps from branch to branch [pause] and chatters and flips its tail when it's excited [pause] . . ."

Finally one little boy tentatively raised his hand. The priest breathed a sigh of relief and called on him. "Well," said the boy, "I know the answer must be Jesus . . . but it sure sounds like a squirrel to me!"

A PRIEST was in the hospital recovering from a heart bypass operation. The chairman of the parish council came to visit and said he brought greetings from the entire council as well as their wishes that he should recover soon and return to the parish.

The priest thanked him and said that was very nice.

The chairman said, "It's more than 'nice.' It was an official resolution . . . passed by a vote of ten to five."

A POLICE officer pulled over a carload of nuns.

Cop: "Sister, this is an eighty kilometre per hour highway—why are you going so slow?"

Sister: "Sir, I saw a lot of signs that said fifty-nine, not eighty."

Cop: "Sister, that's not the speed limit, that's the name of the highway you're on!"

Sister: "Oh! Silly me! Thanks for letting me know. I'll be more careful."

At this point, the cop looked in the back seat where the other nuns were shaking and trembling.

Cop: "Excuse me, Sister, what's wrong with your friends back there? They're shaking something terrible."

Sister: "Oh, we just got off of the 401."

A MAN was leaving church one Sunday, and the priest was standing at the door, as he always was, to shake hands. The homily that day had been about the people of God being in the "Army of the Lord."

The priest shook the man's hand and pulled him aside. "You know, you need to join the Army of the Lord."

The man replied, "I'm already in the Army of the Lord, Father."

The priest asked, "How come I don't see you—except at Christmas and Easter?"

The man whispered, "I'm in the secret service."

"DOES YOUR husband attend church regularly?" the priest asked a woman.

"Oh yes," she answered. "He hasn't missed an Easter or Christmas since we were married."

MANY CHURCHES are now serving coffee after Mass on Sundays. This is supposedly to get the people thoroughly awake before they drive home.

A HEAVY snowstorm closed the schools in a small Ontario town. When the children returned to school a few days later, a grade school teacher asked her students whether they had used the time away from school constructively.

"I sure did, teacher," one little girl replied. "I prayed for more snow."

SURGEON: "I think the medical profession is the first profession mentioned in the Bible. God made Eve by carving a rib out of Adam."

Engineer: "No, engineering was first. Just think of the engineering job it was to create things out of chaos."

Politician: "Who do you think created the chaos?"

A NEW army recruit was given guard duty at two a.m. and fell asleep. He awoke to find the officer of the day standing before him. Knowing the penalty for falling asleep, the young man kept his head bowed for a moment longer, then looked heavenward and said, "A-a-a-men!"

A SUNDAY school teacher asked her class to draw a picture of a Bible story. One paper that was handed in contained a picture of a big car. An old man, with long whiskers flying in the breeze, was driving. A man and a woman were seated in the back seat.

Puzzled, the teacher approached little Johnny and asked him about his drawing.

"Oh that's God. He's driving Adam and Eve out of the Garden of Eden."

A PRIEST was about to baptize a baby. Turning to the father he asked, "What name do you give your child?"

"William Patrick Arthur Timothy Kenneth John MacArthur."

The priest turned to his assistant and said, "A little more water, please."

BILLY: "How do you suppose babies get belly buttons?"

Suzy: "Well, when God finishes making little babies, He lines them all up in a row. Then he walks along in front of them, pokes each one in the tummy with His finger and says, "You're done . . . you're done . . . and you're done."

A YOUNG priest decided he wanted to be a police chaplain, so he took a written examination at the station.

One of the questions was, "What would you do to disperse a frenzied crowd?"

He thought for a moment, then wrote his answer: "I would take up a collection."

THE LOCAL church hired a new choir director for the struggling church choir.

At the time, the church was undergoing roof repairs. As a result, the roof was uncovered, with just the tin foundation exposed.

Meanwhile, the choir director was working with the worst choral voices this side of Rome. On Sunday morning, during the choir director's debut, the choir sounded awful. All of a sudden, a fierce hailstorm broke out, just as the choir was singing its last hymn. The priest stood up, looked toward the rooftop and exclaimed, "It sounds like hail!"

The choir director cried out, "Give me a break! I'm doing the best I can!"

A PRIEST went visiting one afternoon. He knocked on a door several times, but no one answered. He could see through the window that the TV was on, so he took one of his cards and wrote on it, "Revelation 3:20—Behold I stand at the door and knock: if anyone will open I will come in." He stuck the card in the door.

The following Sunday, a woman handed him a card with her name on it and the following message, "Genesis 3:10—I heard your voice, and I was naked—so I hid myself."

A NUN was driving home to the convent from her daily rounds at the local hospital when her car ran out of gas. The only container she had was a large bedpan.

She carried it to the nearest gas station and had it filled with gas. When she returned to her car, she began to pour the gas into the gas tank. Two priests driving by saw what the nun was doing. The older priest said to the younger, "Now, that's absolute faith in the Lord."

A POOR deacon's wife came home with a dress that was very expensive and more than they could afford. The wife admitted that the temptation was more than she could bear, so she bought the dress.

Her husband admonished her. "You should have told Satan to get behind you!"

His wife replied, "I did, and he said it looked marvellous from the back as well."

A DEVOUT Catholic woman was running late to church when she slipped and fell, skinning her elbows and knees, and splitting her skirt.

Dazed and confused, she glanced up and saw a man staring at her from the church steps.

"Are you okay?" he asked.

"Yes, but is Mass out?" she asked.

Looking at her backside, he replied, "No ma'am, but your hat is on crooked."

A PRIEST was asked by a politician, "What can the government do to help the church?"

The priest replied, "Stop making loonies."

A YOUNG woman was collecting for charity on the streets of the city. When she saw an elderly gentlemen approach, she asked him, "Will you give me a loonie for the Lord?"

The elderly gentleman asked her, "How old are you, young lady?"

"I'm twenty-two," she replied.

"I'm eighty-four," he answered. "I am certain that I will see the

Lord before you do, so I'll hang on to my loonie and give it to Him myself!"

TWO SMALL children were sitting together in church. The younger child giggled, sang, and talked out loud. Finally, his big sister scolded him.

"You're not supposed to make noise in church."

"Why? Who's going to stop me?" the younger brother asked.

His sister pointed to the back of the church and said, "See those two men standing on either side of the door? They're hushers."

A DYING woman was getting her affairs in order. She prepared her will and made her final arrangements. As part of these arrangements she met with her parish priest to talk about her funeral. She told him she had only two requests.

First, she wanted to be cremated, and second, she wanted her ashes scattered over the local shopping mall.

"The mall?" the priest asked. "Why the mall?"

"That way, I know my daughters will visit me twice a week."

A CLERGYMAN was walking down a country lane and saw a young farmer struggling to load hay back onto a cart after it had fallen off.

"You look hot, my son," said the cleric. "Why don't you rest a moment, and I'll give you a hand."

"No thanks," said the young man. "My father wouldn't like it."

"Don't be silly," the priest said. "Everyone is entitled to a break. Come and have a drink of water."

Again the young man protested that his father would be upset.

Losing his patience, the clergyman said, "Your father must be a real slave driver. Tell me where I can find him and I'll give him a piece of my mind!"

"He's under the load of hay."

FRED HAD been a faithful Catholic and was in the hospital, near death. The family called their priest to stand with them. As the priest stood next to the bed, Fred's condition appeared to deteriorate and he motioned frantically for something to write on.

The priest lovingly handed him a pen and a piece of paper and Fred used his last bit of energy to scribble a note, then he died.

The priest thought it best not to look at the note at that time, so he placed it in his jacket pocket.

At the funeral, as he was finishing the eulogy, he realized that he was wearing the same jacket that he was wearing when Fred died. He said to the gathering, "You know, Fred handed me a note just before he died. I haven't looked at it, but knowing Fred, I'm sure there's a word of inspiration there for us all."

He opened the note, and read aloud, "Hey, you're standing on my oxygen tube!"

A LOQUACIOUS priest, known for his lengthy sermons, noticed a man get up and leave during the middle of his message. The man returned just before the conclusion of the homily. Afterwards the priest asked the man where he had gone.

"I went to get a haircut," was the reply.

"Why didn't you do that before I started Mass?"

"Because," the gentleman said, "I didn't need one then."

A MAN died and found himself waiting in the long line of judgment. As he stood around he noticed that some souls were allowed to march right through the Gates of Heaven while others were led to Satan, who threw them into the burning pit. But every so often, instead of hurling a poor soul into the fire, Satan would toss a soul off to one side into a small pile.

After watching Satan do this several times, the fellow's curiosity got the better of him. So he strolled over and tapped Satan on the shoulder. "Excuse me," he said. "I'm waiting in line for judgment, but I couldn't help wondering, why are you tossing those people aside instead of flinging them into the fires of hell with the others?"

"Ah, those . . ." Satan said with a groan. "They're from Vancouver. They're too wet to burn!"

AN ELDERLY husband and wife who had been married for sixty years died in a car crash. They had been in good health the last ten years, mainly due to her interest in health food.

When they reached the Pearly Gates, St. Peter took them to their mansion, which was decked out with a beautiful kitchen, master bath suite and a Jacuzzi. As they looked around, the old man asked St. Peter how much all this was going to cost.

"It's free," St. Peter replied. "This is heaven."

Next, they went in the back yard to survey the championship-style golf course on which the home was located. They learned they would have golfing privileges every day and, each week, the course changed to a new one representing the great golf courses on earth. The old man asked, "What are the green fees?"

St. Peter replied, "This is heaven, you play for free."

Next, they went to the clubhouse and saw the lavish buffet lunch with the cuisines of the world laid out. "How much to eat?" asked the old man.

"Don't you understand? This is heaven. Everything is free!" St. Peter replied.

"Well, where are the low fat and low cholesterol tables?" the old man asked, timidly.

St. Peter answered, "That's the best part. You can eat as much as you like of whatever you like and you never get fat and you never get sick. This is heaven!"

The old man turned to his wife and yelled, "If it weren't for your blasted bran muffins, I could have been here ten years ago!"

BEFORE PERFORMING a baptism, the priest approached the young father and said solemnly, "Baptism is a serious step. Are you prepared for it?"

"I think so," the man replied. "My wife has made appetizers and we have a caterer coming to provide plenty of cookies and cakes for all of our guests."

"I don't mean that," the priest responded. "I mean, are you prepared spiritually?"

"Oh, sure," came the reply. "I've got a keg of beer and a case of scotch."

A COUPLE of weeks after hearing a homily about lies and deceit, a man wrote the following letter to the tax department in Ottawa:

"I have been unable to sleep, knowing that I have cheated on my income tax. I understated my taxable income, and have enclosed a check for $150. If I still can't sleep, I will send the rest."

A MAN who was an avid golfer finally got a once-in-a-lifetime chance for an audience with the pope. After standing in line for hours, he got to meet the pope and said, "Holiness, I have a question that only you can answer. You see, I love golf, and I feel a real need to know if there is a golf course in heaven. Can you tell me if there is?"

The pope considered this for a moment, and said, "I do not know the answer to your question, my son, but I will talk to God and get back to you."

The next day, the man was called for another audience with the pope to receive the answer to his question. The pope told him, "My son, I have some good news and some bad news in relation to your question. The good news is that heaven has the most fabulous golf course that you could imagine, and it is in perfect shape for all eternity. It puts all courses on earth to shame. The bad news is that you have a tee-off time for tomorrow morning."

A PATIENT awakened after a serious operation only to find herself in a room with all the blinds drawn.

"Why are all the blinds closed?" she asked her doctor.

"Well," the surgeon responded, "They're fighting a huge fire across the street and we didn't want you to wake up and think the operation had failed."

AT SUNDAY school they were teaching how God created everything, including human beings.

Little Johnny, a child in the kindergarten class, seemed especially intent when they told him how Eve was created out of one of Adam's ribs. Later in the week his mother noticed him lying down as though he were ill, and said, "Johnny what is the matter?"

Little Johnny responded, "I have a pain in my side. I think I'm going to have a wife."

A CORRUPT accountant with a multi-national company fell asleep and dreamed he went to heaven. Upon arriving he noticed there were clocks everywhere. He asked St. Peter, "What's with the clocks?"

St. Peter replied: "Each clock represents one person on earth. Each time they sin, the clock moves forward one minute. For example, this clock, which is moving fairly quickly, belongs to a dishonest used car salesman. And this one here that is barely moving belongs to a pious priest. And this one here with the cobwebs belongs to a saint."

As he continued the tour of clocks, the man asked St. Peter, "What about me, where is my clock?"

St. Peter replied, "God is using it in his office as a fan."

CHAPTER FIVE

"To laugh often and much, to win the respect of intelligent people and the affection of children . . . to leave the world a bit better . . . to know even one life has breathed a little easier because you have lived, that is to have succeeded."

Ralph Waldo Emerson

Father Ray Rick

St. Peter the Apostle
Parry Sound, Ontario

When my wife Kris and I bought recreational lakefront property in 1992 and erected a Confederation Log Home on Manitouwabing Lake, near the north-central Ontario town of McKellar, we were a little disappointed to learn that the nearest Catholic Church was in the town of Parry Sound. After driving two-and-a-half hours from our Richmond Hill home to get to the cottage on Friday nights, we weren't thrilled to drive another hour to and from Mass on summer Sunday mornings. Our letdown was short-lived, however, after we met the parish priest of St. Peter the Apostle. In 1992, he was Australian-born and bred Father Ken Rae, a delightful man with a well-tuned and sharp Aussie humour.

We enjoyed his wonderful sermons and keen wit for many years, until our favourite "Strine" left to study canon law in the U.S. Today, St. Peter's is well represented by Father Ray Rick whose humorous side is every bit as evident as his predecessor's. When I asked Father Ray if he had any funny stories to share with me for God's Jesters, *he said he had "a million of 'em."*

And he wasn't kidding!

Father Ray cut and pasted some jokes from his collection, then e-mailed twenty-seven pages of the better ones to me. What a gold mine of humour! He, too, gets a whole chapter in this book because I want to discourage him from going into pastoral joke book competition with me! Here are just some of his favourites:

> A TEN-YEAR-old boy was failing math. His parents tried everything to get him to do well in school, but nothing worked. Finally, they enrolled him in a Catholic school.
>
> After the first day, the boy's parents were surprised when he walked in after school with a stern, focused and very determined expression on his face. He went straight past them, right to his room and quietly closed the door. For nearly two hours he toiled away at math in his room, books strewn about his desk and the surrounding floor.

He emerged long enough to eat, and after quickly cleaning his plate, went straight back to his room, closed the door and worked feverishly at his studies until bedtime.

This pattern of behaviour continued until it was time for the first quarter's report card. The boy walked in with it unopened, laid it on the dinner table and went straight to his room.

Cautiously, his mother opened it and, to her amazement, she saw a large red "A" under the subject of math. Overjoyed, she and her husband rushed into their son's room, thrilled at his remarkable progress.

"Was it the nuns that did it?" the father asked.

The boy shook his head and said, "No."

"Was it the one-on-one tutoring? The peer-mentoring?"

"No."

"The textbooks? The teachers? The curriculum?"

"No," said the son. "On that first day, when I walked in the front door and saw that guy nailed to the plus sign, I KNEW they were serious!"

A MAN was struck by a bus on a busy street in Toronto. He lay dying on the sidewalk as a crowd of spectators gathered around. "A priest! Somebody get me a priest!" the man gasped.

A policeman checked the crowd but could find no priest, no minister, and no man of God of any kind.

"A PRIEST, PLEASE!" the dying man said again.

Then, out of the crowd stepped a little old Jewish man of at least eighty years of age. "Mr. Policeman," said the man, "I'm not a priest. I'm not even a Catholic. But for fifty years I'm living behind St. Elizabeth's Catholic Church on First Avenue, and every night I'm listening to the Catholic litany. Maybe I can be of some comfort to this man."

The policeman agreed and brought the octogenarian to where the dying man lay. The old man kneeled down, leaned over the injured fellow and said in a solemn voice, "B–4. I–19. N–38. G–54. O–72 . . ."

A PRIEST died and was waiting in line at the Pearly Gates. Ahead of him was a man dressed in sunglasses, a loud shirt, leather jacket and jeans.

St. Peter said to the first man, "Who are you, so that I may know whether or not to admit you to heaven?"

The guy replied, "I'm Joe Smith, taxi driver."

St. Peter checked his list, smiled and said to him, "Take this silken robe and golden staff and enter heaven."

The taxi driver went right to heaven. The priest's turn was next. He stood erect and boomed out in a loud voice, "I am Father Wendell Snow, pastor of Saint Mary's Church for the last forty-three years."

St. Peter checked his list, and then said to the priest, "Take this cotton robe and wooden staff and enter heaven."

"Just a minute," said the priest. "That man was a taxi driver and he got a silken robe and golden staff. How can this be?"

"Up here, we work by results," said St. Peter. "While you preached, people slept; while he drove, people prayed."

SISTER CATHERINE was asking all the Catholic school children in fourth grade what they wanted to be when they grew up. Little Sheila said: "When I grow up, I want to be a prostitute!"

Sister Catherine's eyes grew wide and she yelled, "What? WHAT did you say?"

"A prostitute!" Sheila repeated.

Sister Catherine breathed a sigh of relief and said, "Thank God! I thought you said a *Protestant*!"

A MAN was in bed with his wife when there was a rat-a-tat-tat on the door. He rolled over and looked at his clock. It was half past three in the morning. "I'm not getting out of bed at this time of the morning," he said aloud, and rolled over. Soon, a louder knock followed.

"Aren't you going to answer that?" asked his wife.

The man dragged himself out of bed and went downstairs. He opened the door to see a man standing on the doorstep. It didn't take the homeowner long to realize the man was drunk.

"Hi there," slurred the stranger. "Can you give me a push?"

"No, get lost. It's half past three. I was in bed," said the man as he slammed the door. He went back to bed and told his wife what happened. She said, "Dave, that wasn't very nice of you. Remember that night our car broke down in the pouring rain on the way to pick up the kids from the baby sitter and you had to knock on someone's house to get us going again? What would have happened if they'd told us to get lost?"

"But this guy is drunk," said the husband.

"It doesn't matter," replied the wife. "He needs our help and it would be a Christian thing to help him."

So the husband got out of bed again, got dressed, and went downstairs. He opened the door but couldn't see the stranger anywhere. So, he shouted, "Hey, do you still want a push?"

He heard a voice cry out, "Yeah, please."

Still unable to see the stranger he shouted, "Where are you?"

The stranger replied, "I'm over here, on your swing."

SHERLOCK HOLMES and Dr. Watson went on a camping trip. As they lay down for the night, Holmes said, "Watson, look up into the sky and tell me what you see."

Watson said, "I see millions and millions of stars."

"And what does that tell you?"

"Astronomically," Watson replied, "it tells me that there are millions of galaxies and potentially billions of planets. Theologically, it tells me that God is great and that we are small and insignificant. Meteorologically, it tells me that we will have a beautiful day tomorrow. What does it tell you?"

"You idiot, Watson! Somebody stole our tent!"

AN ELDERLY couple was experiencing declining memory, so they decided to take a power memory class, where they teach you to remember things by association.

A week later, the man was telling a neighbour how much the class helped him.

"Who was the instructor?" asked the neighbour.

"Oh, let's see," pondered the man. "Umm . . . what's that flower, you know, that smells real nice, but it has those thorns . . .?"

"A rose?" offered the neighbour.

"Right," said the man. He turned toward his house and shouted, "Hey, Rose, what's the name of the guy we took that memory class from?"

A DOCTOR saw an old man walking down the street with a gorgeous young lady on his arm! The next time the old man had an appointment, the doctor said, "You're really doing great, aren't you?"

"Just doing what you told me, Doctor. 'Get a hot mamma. Be cheerful.'"

"I didn't say that. I said, 'You've got a heart murmur, be careful!'"

BECAUSE HE lived far away, a man was unable to attend the funeral of his uncle when the uncle died.

He called his brother and told him, "Do something nice for Uncle George and send me the bill." Later, he received a bill for $200, which he paid. A month later, he got another bill for $200, which he also paid, figuring it was some incidental expense. But, when the bills for $200 kept arriving every month, he finally called his brother to find out what was going on.

"You said to do something nice for Uncle George," said the brother. "So, I rented him a tuxedo."

A MIDDLE-aged woman witnessed a most unusual funeral procession. It consisted of two black hearses followed by a woman walking two big dogs, followed by two hundred women walking in single file.

Unable to restrain her curiosity, the middle-aged lady approached the woman with the two dogs and said, "I'm sorry if this is intrusive, but can you tell me what this is all about?"

"Oh, yes," she replied. "That first car contains my husband."

"I'm terribly sorry," the first woman said. "How did he die?"

"He was attacked by these two dogs," the woman said, without much hint of regret in her voice. "And the second hearse contains my mother-in-law. She came upon the scene and attempted to rescue her son, and the dogs turned on her as well."

"I see," said the curious bystander. Then after a solemn moment, "Do you suppose I could borrow those dogs?"

"Get in line."

A GOLFER and his buddies were playing a round of golf with $200 on the line. At the eighteenth green the golfer needed to sink a ten-foot putt to win the round and the $200. As he lined up his putt, a funeral procession passed by. The golfer set down his putter, took off his hat, placed it over his chest, and waited for the funeral procession to go by. After it passed, he picked up his putter and returned to lining up his putt.

One of his buddies said, "That was the most touching thing I have ever seen. I can't believe you stopped playing, possibly losing your concentration, to pay your respects."

The golfer turned to him and said, "Well, it was the least I could do. We were married for forty-five years!"

THE CUSTODIAN of a church quit so the pastor asked the church organist if she would also do the job of cleaning the church sanctuary. The organist thought for a while before she answered, "Do you mean that I now have to mind my keys and pews?"

Children Were Asked: How Do You Decide Whom to Marry?

"You got to find somebody who likes the same stuff. Like if you like sports, she should like it that you like sports, and she should keep the chips and dip coming."

Allan, age 10

"No person really decides before they grow up who they're going to marry. God decides it all way before, and you get to find out later who you're stuck with."

Kirsten, age 10

How Can a Stranger Tell if Two People are Married?

"Married people usually look happy to talk to other people."

Eddie, age 6

"You might have to guess based on whether they seem to be yelling at the same kids."

Derrick, age 8

The Great Debate: Is It Better to be Single or Married?

"Single is better . . . for the simple reason that I wouldn't want to change no diapers . . . Of course, if I did get married, I'd figure something out. I'd just phone my mother and have her come over for some coffee and diaper-changing."

Kirsten, age 10

Question: How many car salesmen does it take to change a light bulb?

Answer: I'm just going to work this out on my calculator and I know you will be pleasantly surprised.

IN AN effort to get parishioners to dispose of the paper towels properly, a pastor placed a sign directly above the sink in the bathroom off the vestibule of the church. It had a single word on it: THINK! The next day someone had carefully lettered another sign just above the soap dispenser that read: THOAP!

DID YOU hear about the Buddhist who refused his dentist's Novocain during root canal work? He wanted to transcend dental medication.

A MAN entered a local paper's pun contest. He sent in ten different puns, in hopes that at least one of the puns would win. Unfortunately, no pun in ten did.

ONE SUMMER evening, during a violent thunderstorm, a mother tucked her small boy into bed. She was about to turn off the light when he asked, with a tremor in his voice, "Mommy, will you sleep with me tonight?"

The mother smiled and gave him a reassuring hug. "I can't, dear," she said. "I have to sleep in Daddy's room." A long silence was broken by his shaky little voice: "Big sissy."

A CHILD came home from Sunday school and told his mother that he had learned a new song about a cross-eyed bear named Gladly.

It took his mother a while before she realized that the hymn was "Gladly the Cross I'd Bear."

CATHOLIC DICTIONARY

Amen: The only part of a prayer that everyone knows.

Bulletin: a) Parish information, read only during the homily. b) Catholic air-conditioning. c) Your receipt for attending Mass.

Choir: A group of people whose singing allows the rest of the congregation to lip-sync.

Holy Water: A liquid whose chemical formula is H_2OLY.

Hymn: A song of praise, usually sung in a key three octaves higher than that of the congregation's range.

Recessional Hymn: The last song at Mass, often sung a little more quietly, since most of the people have already left.

Incense: Holy Smoke!

Jesuits: An order of priests known for their ability to found colleges with good basketball teams.

Jonah: The original "Jaws" story.

Justice: When kids have kids of their own.

Kyrie Eleison: The only Greek words that most Catholics can recognize besides gyros and baklava.

Magi: The most famous trio to attend a baby shower.

Manger: a) Where Mary gave birth to Jesus because Joseph wasn't covered by medical insurance. b) The Bible's way of showing us that holiday travel has always been rough.

Pew: A medieval torture device still found in Catholic churches.

Procession: The ceremonial formation at the beginning of Mass, consisting of altar servers, the celebrant, and late parishioners looking for seats.

Recessional: The ceremonial procession at the conclusion of Mass—led by parishioners trying to beat the crowd to the parking lot.

Relics: People who have been going to Mass for so long, they actually know when to sit, kneel, and stand.

Ten Commandments: The most important Top Ten list not given by David Letterman.

Ushers: The only people in the parish who don't know the seating capacity of a pew.

A NEW convert to Catholicism decided to go to confession to deal with his transgression.

In the confessional, he told the priest that he had sinned.

"What was your sin, my son?" asked the priest.

"I stole some lumber, Father," replied the penitent.

"How much lumber did you steal?" asked the priest.

"I built a new doghouse for my German shepherd."

The priest replied, "Well, that's not so bad."

The penitent interrupted him. "Father, I also built myself a four-car garage."

The priest responded, "Now that's a little more serious!"

The penitent again interrupted the priest. "Father, I've got to get it off my chest. I built a doghouse, a four-car garage, and a five-bedroom home!"

The priest was shocked. He responded, "Well, that is very serious. I'm afraid you'll have to make a novena."

The penitent looked perplexed and then said, "Father, I don't know what a novena is, but if you've got the blueprints, I've got the lumber."

THE TEACHER announced to her class that she was an atheist and asked how many of the children were also atheists. All the students put up their hands, except Judy.

"If you're not an atheist," the teacher asked, "what are you, Judy?"

"I'm a Christian," she answered.

"How do you know you are a Christian?"

"Well," she replied. "My mother is a Christian and my father is also a Christian."

"If both your parents were morons would you be a moron too?" the teacher jeered.

"No," said Judy. "Then I'd be an atheist."

A MAN was standing before St. Peter at the Gates of Heaven. While looking at his large ledger, St. Peter said, "You don't seem to have done anything particularly bad during your lifetime, but then again, you never did anything particularly good for anyone, either."

St. Peter looked at the slight young man before him and said, "If you can tell me of one exceptional good deed you accomplished in your lifetime I'll let you in."

The man said, "No problem! I was driving down the main road of my hometown when I saw a bunch of motorcycle gang members hassling a young lady. I parked my car, got out, grabbed a tire iron and rushed over."

"What happened next?" asked a now-curious St. Peter.

"Well, I went up to the man who was clearly the leader. This guy was big and he was bald. But he had hair everywhere else and had a chain hooked from a ring in his nose to a ring in his ear," the young man continued. "I told him to leave the girl alone or I would club him."

"Go on," said St. Peter.

"Well, then he started to laugh and took a step toward me. I clobbered him with the tire iron and he went down like a ton of bricks. Then I turned to the rest of his gang and said that if they didn't want some of the same they had better take off and leave the girl alone."

"Very impressive," responded St. Peter as he turned the pages of his ledger.

"But I can't seem to find any reference to that in my book. When did this occur?"

"About two minutes ago," replied the young man.

ONE SUNDAY the priest told his congregation the church needed some extra money, so he asked the people to prayerfully consider giving a little extra in the offering plate. He said that whoever gave the most would be permitted to pick out three hymns.

After the offering plates were passed, the pastor glanced down and noticed that someone had placed a $100 bill in offering. He was so excited that he immediately shared his joy with the congregation and said he'd like to personally thank the person who had placed the money in the plate.

An elderly lady in the back shyly raised her hand. The priest asked her to come to the front. Slowly, she made her way toward the pastor. He told her how wonderful it was that she gave so much. In thanksgiving, he asked her to pick out three hymns.

Her eyes brightened as she looked over the congregation and said, "I'll take him, him and him."

AN OLD priest was getting sick and tired of all the people in his parish who kept confessing adultery. One Sunday, from the pulpit, he said, "If I hear one more person confess to adultery, I'll quit."

Everyone liked him and didn't want him to quit, so they came up with a code word. Anyone who had committed adultery would say that they had "fallen."

Things went along quite well until, at a great age, he died. About a week after the new priest arrived he went to see the mayor of the town in a very concerned frame of mind. "You have to do something about the sidewalks in town," he said. "When people come to confession, they keep talking about having 'fallen.'"

The mayor started to laugh, realizing that no one had told the new priest about the code word.

Before the mayor could explain, the priest shook an accusing finger at him and said, "You shouldn't be laughing. Your own wife fell three times last week."

A MAN left the snow-filled streets of Toronto for a vacation in Florida. His wife was on a business trip and was planning to meet him there the next day.

When he reached his hotel, the man decided to send his wife a quick e-mail. He couldn't find the piece of scrap paper on which he had written her e-mail address, so he did his best and typed it from memory. Unfortunately, he missed one letter, and his note was directed instead to an elderly preacher's wife, whose husband had passed away the day before.

When the grieving widow checked her e-mail, she took one look at the monitor, let out a piercing scream, and fell to the floor in a dead faint.

At the sound, her family rushed into the room and saw this note on the screen:

"Dearest Wife,

Just got checked in. Everything prepared for your arrival tomorrow.

P.S. Sure is hot down here."

THE POPE: Leaps tall buildings in a single bound, is more powerful than a locomotive, is faster than a speeding bullet, walks on water and gives policy to God.

The Cardinal: Leaps short buildings in a single bound, is more powerful than a switch engine, just about as fast as a speeding bullet, walks on water if the sea is calm and talks to God.

The Archbishop: Leaps short buildings with a running start and favourable wind, is almost as powerful as a switch engine, is faster than a BB pellet, walks on water in an indoor swimming pool and talks with God if his request is approved.

The Bishop: Barely clears Quonset huts, loses tug-of-war with locomotives, can fire a speeding bullet, swims well and is sometimes addressed by God.

The Monsignor: Makes high marks on walls when trying to leap tall buildings, is run over by locomotives, can sometimes handle a gun without inflicting self-injury, dog paddles and talks to animals.

The Pastor: Runs into buildings, recognizes locomotives two times out of three, is not issued ammunition, can stay afloat with a life preserver and talks to himself.

The Associate Pastor: Falls over the doorstep to buildings, says, "Look at the choo-choo" when he sees a train, wets himself with a water pistol and babbles incoherently.

The Church Secretary: Lifts tall buildings and walks under them, kicks locomotives off the track, catches speeding bullets in her teeth and eats them, freezes water with a single glance, and is next to God!

A WOMAN and her son went to church on Sunday morning. She gave him a quarter to put in the collection.

When the plate came around, she noticed he did not put it in. When they got home she lectured him about learning to give, and ordered him to get on his bicycle and go back to the church, find the priest and give him the quarter.

The boy got on his bicycle, went back to the church and found the priest still putting things away. He said, "Father, I want you to have this quarter."

The priest said, "Thank you very much. The collection is right over there, just drop it in."

The boy replied, "Oh, no, Father, I want you to have it. My mom says you're the poorest priest we've ever had."

A WOMAN approached a priest and told him, "Father, I have a problem. I inherited two talking female parrots, but they only know how to say one thing."

"What do they say?" the priest asked.

"They only know how to say, 'Hi, we're prostitutes. Do you want to have some fun?'"

"That's terrible!" the priest exclaimed. "However, I have a solution to your problem. Bring your two talking female parrots to my house and I will put them with my two male talking parrots that I have taught to pray and read the Bible. My parrots will teach your parrots to stop saying that terrible phrase and your female parrots will learn to pray and worship."

"Thank you," said the woman.

The next day, the woman brought her female parrots to the priest's house. The priest's two male parrots were holding rosary beads and praying in their cage.

The woman put her female talking parrots in with the male parrots and the female parrots said, "Hi, we're prostitutes! Do you want to have some fun?"

One male parrot looked at the other male parrot and said, "Put your rosary away, Frank, our prayers have been answered!"

DAVID RECEIVED a parrot for his birthday. The parrot was fully grown, with a bad attitude and worse vocabulary. Every other word was an expletive. Those that weren't expletives were, to say the least, rude.

David tried hard to change the bird's attitude and was constantly saying polite words, playing soft music, anything that came to mind. Nothing worked. He yelled at the bird, the bird got worse. He shook the bird and the bird got madder and ruder. Finally, in a moment of desperation, David put the parrot in the freezer. For a few moments he heard the bird squawking, kicking and screaming and then, suddenly, all was quiet.

David was frightened that he might have actually hurt the bird and quickly opened the freezer door. The parrot calmly stepped out onto David's extended arm and said, "I'm sorry that I offended you with my language and actions. I ask for your forgiveness. I will try to check my behaviour."

David was astounded at the bird's change in attitude and was about to ask what changed him, when the parrot continued, "May I ask what the chicken did?"

A BURGLAR broke into a house one night. He shined his flashlight around, looking for valuables. When he picked up a CD player to place in his sack, a strange, disembodied voice echoed from the darkness saying, "Jesus is watching you."

He nearly jumped out of his skin, turned his flashlight off and froze. He heard nothing more. After a while he shook his head and promised himself a vacation after the next big score, then clicked the light back on and began searching for more valuables. Just as he started to disconnect the wires of the stereo, he again heard the words, "Jesus is watching you."

Freaked out, he shined his light around frantically, looking for the source of the voice. Finally, in the corner of the room, the beam of the flashlight came to rest on a parrot.

"Did you say that?" the burglar hissed at the parrot.

"Yep," the parrot confessed, then squawked, "I'm just trying to warn you."

The burglar relaxed. "Warn me, huh? Who in the world are you?"

"Moses" replied the bird.

"Moses?" the burglar laughed. "What kind of a stupid person would name a parrot Moses?"

The bird answered, "The same kind of stupid person that would name a Rottweiler 'Jesus.'"

THINGS WE CAN LEARN FROM A DOG

When loved ones come home, always run to greet them.

When it's in your best interest, practise obedience.

Let others know when they invade your territory.

Take naps, and stretch before rising.

Eat with gusto and enthusiasm.

Be loyal.

When something you want is buried, dig until you find it.

When someone is having a bad day, be silent, sit close by and nuzzle him or her gently.

Avoid biting when a simple growl will do.

No matter how often you are scolded, don't dwell on guilt . . . run right back and make friends.

A MORNING PRAYER

Dear God,
So far today,
I haven't gossiped.
I haven't lost my temper.
I haven't lied or cheated.
I haven't been greedy, grumpy, nasty,
selfish or overindulgent.
I'm very thankful for that.
But in a few minutes, Lord,
I'm going to get out of bed,
and from then on, I'm probably
going to need a lot more help.
Amen.

CHAPTER SIX

"There are three things which are real: God, human folly, and laughter. The first two are beyond our comprehension, so we must do what we can with the third."

John F. Kennedy

Friends, Colleagues and Other Funny Folk

Many of my friends and colleagues from all over the world who are not priests also contributed to this book. People like former British Airways navigator Leo Murphy, from Haywards Heath, Sussex, England; my cousin Brian Cahill's wife, Dianne, from Columbia, South Carolina; good friends Maureen and Jim Mitchell from Markham, Ontario; Marg Scott, Tim Scammell, Brian Currie, Steve McCabe, Peggy Quilty, Lyn Sutherland, and many, many more.

Some of the jokes are old and well worn; others, hilarious side-splitters; still others are off-the-cuff quips. An example of the latter kind occurred in the summer of 2002. I was having dinner with a group of colleagues, all members of the Periodical Writers Association of Canada (PWAC). At the table was a very funny lady, writer/broadcaster Julia Matusky, of Roxboro, Quebec. Next to her was author Mark Kearney, of London, Ontario. Mark is perhaps best known for his Great Canadian Trivia books, but when I learned that he and I were both altar boys in our youth, we shared a few funny stories.

As the evening progressed, the group began talking about what it was like to attend a Catholic school several decades ago. I revealed that one of my teachers in St. Hubert, Quebec, a Sister Jeanne Mance, used to make me sit on just one-half of my chair in school. That allowed my Guardian Angel to sit on the other half of my chair. I agreed it made for an uncomfortable time in the classroom. Mark asked if my Guardian Angel had a name. Before I could reply, Julia answered, "Yeah, Big Butt!"

Here are some of the other contributions from my friends, family and associates:

Man: "Why did Moses wander in the desert for forty years?"

Woman: "Because he wouldn't stop and ask for directions!"

JIM WENT to confession. "Father, I've sinned. I used the Lord's name while playing golf."

"I understand, my son," said the priest. "I play the game myself. Tell me what happened."

"It was the seventeenth hole. I teed off and hit the ball 240 yards right down the middle of the fairway, but it bounced off a sprinkler head and rolled into the woods."

"Is that when you swore?"

"No, Father. I hit a great shot out of the rough, but it landed deep in the sand trap."

"Ah, that's when you took the Lord's name in vain."

"No," said Jim. "I hit the ball perfectly out of the trap, and it ended just four inches from the cup."

"Is that when you blasphemed?" asked the priest.

" No . . ."

The priest replied, "God damn! Don't tell me you missed a four-inch putt!"

ATTEMPTING TO tee off, a priest missed the ball altogether. Red-faced, he looked up at his caddie and mumbled, "Oops." He carefully took another swing, but overcorrected and hit the ground slightly ahead of the ball, bending his best club.

His caddie heard him carefully whisper, "Well, my goodness."

The duffer priest took out another club, rechecked his stance and sliced the ball straight into a tree. The ball bounced right back and walloped him in the forehead. "That's it!" he shouted. "I quit!"

"You're gonna quit golf?" The caddie asked.

"No," replied the golfer. "The priesthood."

A PRIEST was mending the fence behind the rectory when he noticed a neighbour's son paying close attention to the job. "Getting some pointers on mending fences?" the priest asked.

"No, Father," the boy replied. "I'm just waiting to hear what a priest says when he smashes his thumb with a hammer."

AS A storm raged, the captain realized his ship was sinking fast. "Does anyone here know how to pray?" he called out.

One man stepped forward. "Yes, Captain. I know how to pray."

"Good," said the captain. "You pray while the rest of us put our life jackets on. We're one short."

THREE PRIESTS got together over a beer one day and found that all of their churches had an infestation of bats.

"I got so mad," said one priest, "I took a shotgun and fired at them. It made holes in the ceiling, but I didn't hit a single bat."

"I tried trapping them alive," said the second priest. "Then I drove 100 kilometres before releasing them, but they beat me back to the church."

"I haven't had any more problems," said the third priest.

"What did you do?" said the others in amazement.

"I simply baptized them and confirmed them," he replied. "I haven't seen them since."

A VERY rich man was determined to "take it all with him" so he prayed until the Lord finally gave in. There was one condition. He could take only one suitcase of his wealth with him. The rich man decided he would fill the case with gold bullion.

The day came when God called him home. St. Peter greeted him but told him he couldn't bring his suitcase. "But I have an agreement with God," he explained.

"That's unusual," said St. Peter. "Mind if I take a look?" The man opened the suitcase to reveal the shining gold bullion.

St. Peter was amazed. "Why in the world would you bring pavement?"

DID YOU hear about the atheist who turned Catholic because he was tired of the silence every time he sneezed?

A PRIEST went into a barbershop, got a haircut and asked how much he owed. "No charge, Father," the barber said. "I consider it a service to the Lord."

When the barber arrived at the shop the next morning, he found a dozen small prayer books on the front step along with a thank-you note from the priest.

A few days later a police officer came in. "How much do I owe you?" the cop asked after his haircut. "No charge, Officer," said the barber. "I consider it a service to my town."

The next morning the barber found a dozen doughnuts on the step of his barbershop, along with a thank-you note from the police officer.

Several days later, a politician walked in for a haircut. "How much do I owe you?" he asked afterwards. "No charge," said the barber. "I consider it a service to my country."

The next morning when he arrived at the shop, the barber found a dozen more politicians on the front step.

THE ONLY barber in the village was known for his arrogant, know-it-all, negative and argumentative attitude.

When one of his customers mentioned he'd be going to Rome for a vacation, the barber's reaction was typical. "Well, you gotta stay at the Intercontinental Hotel. That's where I always stay. Tell them I sent you."

When he asked his customer what airline he was flying on, the man said Air Canada. "Naw, I always fly Air Italia. Give them my name," said the barber.

When the customer said he hoped to meet the pope, the barber scoffed. "You?" he said. "Meet the pope? Don't make me laugh. The pope sees kings and presidents. Why would he want to see you?"

Three weeks later, the man returned for another haircut. "How was Rome?" asked the barber.

"Great! I met with the pope."

"What? You're kidding! How'd that happen?"

"I was standing in St. Peter's Square with the rest of the crowd when two Swiss guards came up to me and said the pope wanted to meet some people. They took me right into his private apartment in the Vatican."

"Wow!" exclaimed the incredulous barber. "What'd he say?"

"He wanted to know who gave me the lousy haircut."

A COUPLE was desperate to conceive a child, so they went to their priest and asked him to pray for them. "I'm going to live in Rome for a while," he told them. "While I'm there, I'll light a candle for you."

When the priest returned four years later, he visited the couple at their home and found the wife pregnant. She was busy looking after two sets of twins.

The priest was ecstatic. He asked where her husband was so he could offer his congratulations.

"He's in Rome," replied the frazzled mother. "He went to blow out that candle!"

A CALGARY oilman died and went to heaven. At the Gate, St. Peter asked, "What have you done all your life?"

When the man stated his occupation, St. Peter explained there was a surplus of oil executives in heaven. "May I stay if I get rid of the others?" the man asked.

Curious, St. Peter agreed to the unusual request. Once inside the Gates of Heaven, the businessman wandered around until he saw a few familiar faces. He whispered there was an oil strike in hell. Soon, the place was empty of oilmen.

But a while later, the oilman asked St. Peter for permission to leave. "Even though I started the rumour," he said, "there might be something to it."

DURING A court case, a man was giving such unbelievable testimony that the judge warned him he was in danger of perjuring himself.

The judge asked him, "Are you aware of what will happen to you if you are caught lying under oath?"

"Yes, your Honour," replied the witness. "I'll go to hell when I die."

"But what else?" prodded the judge.

"You mean there's more?"

AN AMERICAN, a Scot, and a Canadian were killed in a car accident. When they arrived at the Gates of Heaven, a visibly upset St. Peter explained that there had been a mistake. They weren't supposed to be dead. "Give me $500 each and I will return you to earth as if nothing happened," he said.

"All right!" said the American, and handed over his $500. Immediately, he found himself at the scene of the accident, uninjured.

"Where are the others?" asked the ambulance attendant.

"The last I knew," said the American, "the Scot was haggling over the price and the Canadian was arguing that the government should pay."

TWO NUNS were driving down a back road of Transylvania when a vampire appeared directly in front of their car. The driver yelled, "What should I do? What should I do?"

"Speed up and swerve the car from side to side," screamed her passenger.

They veered and lurched down the highway at 130 km/h, but the vampire was now on the front hood of the car and hanging on for dear life.

"What should I do now?" screamed the nun.

"Hit the brakes," said her colleague.

She did but the vampire remained glued to the windshield.

"Show him your cross! Show him your cross!"

The nun rolled down her window, stuck her head out, and screamed angrily, "Get off my windshield!"

TWO FRIENDS met in heaven one day. George asked Henry how he died. "I froze to death," Henry said.

Then George told his story: "I was at work one day when someone told me that my wife was cheating on me. I rushed home and searched every corner, every room, and every cupboard, under the beds, in closets—everywhere. But I couldn't find anybody. I got so worked up that I had a heart attack and died."

"You should have looked in the freezer," Henry said. "We'd both be alive today."

SISTER URSULA was sitting by the window in her convent one day when she opened a letter from home and found a $10 bill inside. As she read the letter, she noticed a shabbily dressed stranger on the street below. She found a sheet of paper and wrote, "Don't despair. Sister Ursula."

She wrapped the $10 bill in the sheet of paper and dropped it out the window.

The destitute man picked it up and, with a puzzled expression and a tip of his hat, went off down the street.

The next day, Sister Ursula was told that a man was at the door, insisting on seeing her. She went to the lobby and found the stranger waiting. Without saying anything, he handed her a wad of money. "What's this?" she asked.

"That's the $60 you have coming to you. Don't Despair paid five to one!"

JOE AND GARY were rich and evil brothers who attended the same church. When Gary died, Joe handed the pastor a large cheque to pay for a fancy new building.

"I have only one condition," Joe growled. "During his funeral, you must say my brother was a saint."

The pastor agreed and deposited the cheque.

At the funeral, he went to the pulpit and declared, "Gary was an evil man who cheated on his wife and betrayed his friends. But compared to Joe, Gary was a saint."

THE NEW priest was nervous about hearing confessions, so he asked the older priest to sit in on his sessions.

The new priest heard a couple of confessions, then the old priest asked him to step out of the confessional for a little talk.

The old priest suggested, "Cross your arms over your chest, and rub your chin with one hand." The new priest tried this. The old priest then suggested, "Try saying things like, 'I see . . . yes . . . go on,' and, 'I understand' or, 'How did you feel about that?'"

The new priest practised saying those things in front of his mentor.

Then the old priest said, "Now, don't you think that's a little better than slapping your knee and saying, 'No kidding! What happened next?'"

A MAN goes to see a rabbi. "Rabbi, something terrible is happening and I have to talk to you about it."

The rabbi asked, "What's wrong?"

The man replied, "My wife is poisoning me."

The rabbi, very surprised, asked, "How can that be?"

The man pleaded, "I'm just telling you, I'm certain she's poisoning me! What should I do?"

The rabbi thought about it. "Tell you what. Let me talk to her, I'll see what I can find out and I'll let you know."

A week later the rabbi called the man and said, "Well, I spoke to your wife. I spoke to her on the phone for three hours. You want my advice?"

The man anxiously said, "Yes!"

"Take the poison!"

THE PRIEST was preparing a man for his long day's journey into night.

The priest said, in a firm whisper, "Denounce the devil! Let him know how little you think of his evil!"

The dying man said nothing.

The priest repeated his order. Still the dying man said nothing.

The priest asked, "Why do you refuse to denounce the devil and his evil?"

The dying man said, "Until I know where I'm heading, I don't think I ought to aggravate anybody!"

TWO PREACHERS and a rabbi went fishing at the lake. The first preacher said, "I forgot my bait." He then bowed his head, said a prayer, got out of the boat and walked across the water to get some bait from the shore. He then walked back.

The second preacher announced that he had to go to the bathroom. He bowed his head, said a prayer, and then walked across the water to a porta-potty. He walked back to the boat when he was finished.

The rabbi said, "I've got to get something to drink." He bowed his head, said a prayer, got out of the boat, and fell into the water. He nearly drowned before the two preachers pulled him out. One said, "Next time don't try to guess. Just ask one of us where the damn rocks are."

THREE PARISH priests who were having lunch one day decided they could trust each other enough to confess their worst vices.

The first priest said, "I'm ashamed to admit that sometimes I take money from the offering."

The other two priests gasped in shock at the revelation. After recovering, the second admitted, "I must confess that I am carrying on an affair with the wife of one of the parish elders."

Again, the other two reacted with shock.

After wiping his brow, the third priest said with a quiver in his voice, "I must admit to you my brothers, that my worst vice is the sin of gossip and I can't wait to get back to the parish."

A MINISTER and a priest were discussing their respective collection boxes and how the money was split. The priest said, "We give four-fifths to Christian charities and the last fifth we keep for ourselves and for the upkeep of the vicarage."

The minister said, "Each week, my wife and my two children put all the money into the middle of a table. We each take one corner of the tablecloth and we toss the money very high into the air, up to God. Whatever He wants, he takes. The money that falls back to earth we keep!"

A PRIEST and a rabbi operated a church and a synagogue across the street from each other. They decided to pool their money and buy a car together, since it was convenient and their congregations were poor.

After they purchased a car, they drove it home and parked it on the street between them.

A few minutes later, the rabbi looked out and saw the priest sprinkling water on their new car. It didn't need a wash, so he hurried out and asked the priest what he was doing. "I'm blessing it," the priest replied.

The rabbi considered this for a moment, and then went back inside the synagogue. He reappeared a moment later with a hacksaw, walked over to the back of the car and cut two inches off the tailpipe.

AFTER QUASIMODO'S death, the bishop of the Cathedral of Notre Dame sent word through the streets of Paris that a new bell ringer was needed.

The bishop decided that he would conduct the interviews personally, and went up into the belfry to begin the screening process. After observing several applicants demonstrate their skills, he decided to call it a day when a lone, armless man approached him and announced that he was there to apply for the bell ringer's job.

The bishop was incredulous. "You have no arms!"

"No matter," said the man, "Observe, if you will!" He then began striking the bells with his face, producing a beautiful melody on the carillon.

The bishop listened in astonishment, convinced that he had finally found a suitable replacement for Quasimodo. Suddenly, rushing forward to strike a bell, the armless man tripped, and plunged headlong out of the belfry window to his death in the street below.

The stunned bishop rushed to his side. When he reached the street, a crowd had gathered around the fallen figure, drawn by the beautiful music they had heard only moments before. As they silently parted to let the bishop through, one them asked, "Bishop, who was this man?"

"I don't know his name," the bishop sadly replied, "but his face rings a bell."

The following day, despite the sadness that weighed heavily on his heart due to the unfortunate death of the armless campanologist, the bishop continued his interviews for the bell ringer of Notre Dame.

The first man to approach him said, "Your Excellency, I am the brother of the poor, armless wretch that fell to his death from this very belfry yesterday. I pray that you honour his life by allowing me to replace him in this duty."

The bishop agreed to give the man an audition, and as the armless man's brother stooped to pick up a mallet to strike the first bell, he groaned, clutched at his chest and died on the spot. Two monks, hearing the bishop's cries of grief at this second tragedy, rushed up the stairs to his side.

"What has happened?" the first monk breathlessly asked. "Who is this man?"

"I don't know his name," sighed the distraught bishop, "but he's a dead ringer for his brother."

The following announcements actually appeared in various church bulletins:

- Don't let worry kill you—let the church help.
- Remember in prayer the many who are sick of our church and community.
- For those of you who have children and don't know it, we have a nursery downstairs.
- The rosebud on the altar this morning is to announce the birth of David Alan Belzer, the sin of Rev. and Mrs. Julius Belzer.
- This afternoon there will be a meeting in the south and north ends of the church. Children will be baptized at both ends.
- Tuesday at 4:00 p.m. there will be an ice cream social. All ladies giving milk will please come early.
- Wednesday the ladies liturgy will meet. Mrs. Johnson will sing "Put Me in My Little Bed" accompanied by the pastor.
- Thursday at 5:00 p.m. there will be a meeting of the Little Mothers Club. All ladies wishing to be "Little Mothers" will meet with the pastor in his study.
- This being Easter Sunday, we will ask Mrs. Lewis to come forward and lay an egg on the altar.

- The service will close with "Little Drops of Water." One of the ladies will start quietly and the rest of the congregation will join in.
- Next Sunday a special collection will be taken to defray the cost of the new carpet. All those wishing to do something on the new carpet will come forward and do so.

MANY YEARS ago, after watching sales fall off for three straight months at Kentucky Fried Chicken, The Colonel called the pope and asked for a favour. The pope said, "What can I do for you?"

The Colonel said, "I want you to change the daily prayer from, 'Give us this day our daily bread' to 'Give us this day our daily chicken.' If you do it, I'll donate $10 million to the Vatican."

The pope replied, "I am sorry. That is the Lord's Prayer and I cannot change the words." So The Colonel hung up.

After another month of dismal sales, The Colonel panicked, and called again. "Listen, Your Holiness. I really need your help. I'll donate $50 million if you change the words of the daily prayer from 'Give us this day our daily bread' to 'Give us this day our daily chicken.'"

The pope responded, "It is very tempting, Colonel Sanders. The church could do a lot of good with that much money. It would help us to support many charities. But, again, I must decline. It is the Lord's Prayer and I can't change the words."

So The Colonel gave up again. But after two more months of terrible sales, The Colonel got desperate. "This is my final offer, your Holiness. If you change the words of the daily prayer from, 'Give us this day our daily bread' to 'Give us this day our daily chicken' I will donate $100 million to the Vatican."

The pope replied, "Let me get back to you."

The next day, the pope called together all of his bishops and he said, "I have some good news and I have some bad news. The good news is that KFC is going to donate $100 million to the Vatican." The bishops rejoiced at the news.

One of the bishops asked about the bad news.

The pope replied, "The bad news is that we lost the Wonder Bread account."

RANDY AND Dan hadn't seen each other for over a year. They bumped into each other after a football game.

Randy asked, "And how's your wife?"

Dan: "My wife has gone to heaven."

Randy: "Oh, I'm so sorry." Realizing that wasn't the appropriate response, Randy countered by saying, "I guess I mean I'm glad." That didn't sound quite right either so he changed it, saying, "I mean, I'm so surprised!"

He then left the room with both feet in his mouth.

FATHER MURPHY walked into a pub in Donegal, and said to the first man he met, "Do you want to go to heaven?"

The man said, "I do, Father."

The priest said, "Then stand over there against the wall."

Then the priest asked the second man, "Do you want to go to heaven?"

"Certainly, Father," was the man's reply.

"Then stand over there against the wall," said the priest.

Then Father Murphy walked up to O'Toole and said, "Do you want to go to heaven?"

O'Toole said, "No, I don't, Father."

The priest said, "I don't believe this. You mean to tell me that when you die you don't want to go to heaven?"

O'Toole said, "Oh, when I die, yes. I thought you were getting a group together to go right now."

A MAN walking along a California beach was deep in prayer. All of a sudden, he said out loud, "Lord grant me one wish."

The sky clouded above his head and in a booming voice, the Lord said, "Because you have tried to be faithful to me in all ways, I will grant you one wish."

The man said, "Build a bridge to Hawaii, so I can drive over anytime I want."

The Lord said, "Your request is very materialistic. Think of the enormous challenges for that kind of undertaking. The supports required to reach the bottom of the Pacific! The concrete and steel it would take! I can do it, but it is hard for me to justify your desire for worldly things. Take a little more time and think of another wish; a wish you think would honour and glorify me."

The man thought about it for a long time. Finally he said, "Lord, I wish that I could understand women. I want to know how they feel inside, what they are thinking when they give me the silent treatment, why they cry, what they mean when they say 'nothing' and how I can make a woman truly happy."

The Lord replied, "Do you want two lanes or four lanes on that bridge?"

THE WISE old Mother Superior was dying. The nuns gathered around her bed, trying to make her comfortable. They gave her some warm milk to drink, but she refused it.

Then, one nun took the glass back to the kitchen. Remembering a bottle of whisky received as a gift the previous Christmas, she opened it and poured a generous amount onto the warm milk. Back at Mother Superior's bed, she held the glass to her lips. Mother drank a little, and then a little more, then before they knew it, she had drunk the whole glass, down to the last drop.

"Mother, Mother," the nuns cried, "Give us some wisdom before you die."

She raised herself up in bed with a pious look on her face and, pointing out the window, she said, "Don't sell that cow."

Patti Kennedy has been secretary at St. Alphonsus Parish in Whitbourne, Newfoundland & Labrador, since 1987. During that time she said she has seen many humorous and unusual things happen. "I think, in such trying times in our world, it is good to know that a funny story still makes a person forget his or her troubles," she wrote to me. "Even if it's just for a little while. Writing God's Jesters *is a wonderful thing to do, and I hope you will allow my little contribution to be part of it."*

Here's Patti's favourite story:

AT ONE time, we had a priest at our parish that owned two cats. The cats were definitely the masters of the house, and on occasion got into places that got them into trouble.

One day, our priest had a meeting with the ministers of the other faiths in our community to discuss ecumenical service. During the meeting, the topic of people helping in ministries came up and our priest had said earlier that he had been working with two of our parishioners, preparing them to be installed as Eucharistic ministers. As he spoke, one of the other ministers came into the room and said, "I believe your Eucharistic ministers are here for rehearsal!"

When our priest came out of the room, he was horrified to see the two cats coming down the stairs with bags of hosts in their mouths! The breads were always stored upstairs in the study as the parish house was old, and was nice and cool for storing breads and wine.

Lyn Sutherland, of Hamilton, described herself to me as "a very ancient, retired, female doctor." When she read an article in The Catholic Register *about my* God's Jesters *project, she wrote, "I hope you don't mind hearing from a female non-priest." She added, "I became a doctor late in life, after having a family and then working for the Canadian Red Cross Blood Transfusion Service in Hamilton, Ontario, from 1953 to 1956." Lyn acknowledged that some pretty funny (and sometimes outrageous) things happened to her in Hamilton. Here are a few of her favourite, personal stories:*

THE RED Cross used to send a crew out to take blood in various areas of southwestern Ontario. One day, after being away for a week, I met our pastor on the street. Now, this pastor was a very holy man whose beautiful soul was reflected in a gentle, prayerful face. He had lovely soft grey hair and spoke quietly. "Where have you been, Lyn? I haven't seen you around for days."

"I just got back from Guelph," I said. "When I was there, I took blood from seven Jesuits."

Father lifted his head and looked toward heaven with those soulful eyes and said in a pious voice, "Ah! Many of us have wished for a similar opportunity."

TWO BOYS in the area aged ten and twelve were at school, next to the church, where the children were being checked over by the nuns before walking in procession to the church for Confirmation.

A sweet old nun came up to them and complimented them on their appearance. "Are you brothers?" she asked.

The youngest boy was puzzled by the question and replied, "Yes, but only for the past ten years."

Another reader of The Catholic Register, *Peggy Quilty, of Petawawa, Ontario, took time out from caring for her toddler son (and husband) to send me this favourite joke of hers:*

FATHER O'MALLEY got up one fine, spring day and walked to the window of his bedroom to take a deep breath from the beautiful day outside, and noticed there was a jackass lying dead in the middle of his front lawn. He promptly called the local police station.

The conversation went like this: "Top o' the day to ye. This is Sergeant Flaherty. How might I help ye?"

"And the rest of the day te yerself. This is Father O'Malley at St. Brigid's. There's a jackass lying dead in me front lawn. Would ye be after sending a couple o' yer lads to take care of the matter?"

Sgt. Flaherty considered himself to be quite a wit, and the rest of the conversation proceeded: "Well now, Father, it was always my impression that you people took care of last rites!"

There was dead silence on the line for a moment, and then Father O'Malley replied, "Aye, that's certainly true, but we are also obliged to notify the next of kin!"

A LOCAL priest and pastor stood by the side of the road holding up a sign that said, "The End is Near! Turn yourself around NOW before it's too late!"

They planned to hold up the sign to any passing car.

"Leave us alone, you religious nuts!" screamed the first driver as he sped by.

From around the curve they heard a big "splash!"

"Do you think," said one clergy to another, "that we should just put up a sign that says 'bridge out'?"

TIMMY WAS a five-year-old boy whom his mom loved very much and, being a worrier, she was concerned about him walking to school when he started kindergarten.

She walked him to school for a couple of days, but when he came home one day, he told his mother that he did not want her walking him to school every day. He wanted to be like the "big boys." He protested loudly, so she had an idea of how to handle it.

She asked a neighbour, Mrs. Goodnest, if she would surreptitiously follow her son to school, at a distance behind him that he would not likely notice, but close enough to keep a watch on him. Mrs. Goodnest said that since she was up early with her toddler anyway, it would be a good way for them to get some exercise as well, so she agreed.

The next school day, Mrs. Goodnest and her little girl, Marcy, set out following behind Timmy as he walked to school with another neighbour boy he knew. She did this for the entire week.

As the boys walked and chatted, kicking stones and twigs, Timmy's little friend noticed that this same lady was following them as she had seemed to do every day all week. Finally, he said to Timmy, "Have you noticed that lady following us all week? Do you know her?"

Timmy nonchalantly replied, "Yeah, I know who she is."

The little friend said, "Well, who is she?"

"That's just Shirley Goodnest," Timmy said.

"Shirley Goodnest? Who the heck is she and why is she following us?"

"Well," Timmy explained, "every night my mom makes me say the 23rd Psalm with my prayers 'cuz she worries about me so much. And in it, the prayer says, 'Shirley Goodnest and Marcy shall follow me all the days of my life.' So . . . I guess I'll just have to get used to it!"

AN EXASPERATED mother whose son was always getting into mischief finally asked him, "How do you expect to get into heaven?"

The boy thought it over and said, "Well, I'll run in and out and in and out and keep slamming the door until St. Peter says, 'For heaven's sake, Dylan, come in or stay out!'"

THERE WAS a tradesman—a painter—called Jock, who was very interested in making an extra dollar wherever he could, so he often would thin down paint to make it go a wee bit further.

As it happened, he got away with this for some time, but eventually the Bethel Baptist Church in East Wenatchee decided to do a big restoration job on the painting of one of their biggest buildings. Jock put in a bid, and because his price was so low, he got the job.

And so he set to erecting the trestles and setting up the planks, and buying the paint and, yes, I am sorry to say, thinning it down with turpentine.

Well, Jock was up on the scaffolding, painting away, the job nearly completed, when suddenly there was a horrendous clap of thunder, the sky opened, and the rain poured down, washing the thinned paint from all over the church and knocking Jock clear off the scaffold to land on the lawn among the gravestones, surrounded by telltale puddles of the thinned and useless paint.

Jock was no fool. He knew this was a judgment from the Almighty, so he got on his knees and cried, "Oh, God! Forgive me! What should I do?"

And from the thunder, a mighty voice spoke, "Repaint! Repaint! And thin no more!"

AN AMERICAN decided to write a book about famous churches around the world. For his first chapter he decided to write about American churches. So he bought a plane ticket and took a trip to Orlando, thinking that he would work his way across the country from south to north.

On his first day he was inside a church taking photographs when he noticed a golden telephone mounted on the wall with a sign that read "$10,000 per call." The American, being intrigued, asked a priest who was strolling by what the telephone was used for. The priest replied that it was a direct line to heaven and that for $10,000 you could talk to God. The American thanked the priest and went along his way.

Next stop was in Atlanta. There, at a very large cathedral, he saw the same golden telephone with the same sign under it. He wondered if this was the same kind of telephone he saw in Orlando, and he asked a nearby nun what its purpose was. She told him that it was a direct line to heaven and that for $10,000 he could talk to God. "Okay, thank you," said the American.

He then travelled to Indianapolis, Washington, D.C., Philadelphia, Boston, and New York. In every church he saw the same golden telephone with the same "$10,000 per call" sign under it.

The American, upon leaving Vermont, saw a sign for Canada and decided to see if Canadians had the same phone. He arrived in Montreal, and again, there was the same golden telephone, but this time the sign under it read "25 cents per call." The American was surprised so he asked the priest about the sign. "Father, I've travelled all over America and I've seen this same golden telephone in many churches. I'm told that it is a direct line to heaven, but in every state the price was $10,000 per call. Why is it so cheap here?"

The priest smiled and answered, "You're in Canada now, son. It's a local call."

AN ATHEIST was taking a walk through the woods, admiring all that the "accident of evolution" had created.

"What majestic trees! What powerful rivers! What beautiful animals!" he thought to himself.

As he was walking alongside the river he heard a rustling in the bushes behind him. He turned to look. He saw a seven-foot grizzly bear charge toward him. He ran as fast as he could up the path. He looked over his shoulder and saw that the bear was closing in. He ran even faster, so scared that tears were coming to his eyes. He looked over his shoulder again, and the bear was even closer. His heart was pumping frantically and he tried to run even faster. He tripped and fell on the ground. He rolled over to pick himself up but saw the bear, right on top of him, reach for him with his left paw and raise his right paw to strike him.

At that instant the atheist cried out, "Oh, my God!"

Time stopped. The bear froze. The forest was silent. Even the river stopped moving. As a bright light shone upon the man, a voice came out of the sky, "You have denied my existence all these years; taught others that I don't exist; and even credited creation to a cosmic accident. Do you expect me to help you out of this predicament? Am I to count you as a believer . . . NOW?"

The atheist looked directly into the light, "It would be hypocritical of me to suddenly ask you to treat me as a Christian now, but perhaps could you make the bear a Christian?"

"Very well," said the voice.

The light went out. The river ran again. And the sounds of the forest resumed. And then the bear dropped his right paw . . . brought both paws together . . . bowed his head and said, "Lord, for this food which I am about to receive, I am truly thankful."

A NEW monk arrived at the monastery. He was assigned to help the other monks in copying the old texts by hand. He noticed, however, that they were copying from copies, not the original manuscripts.

So, the new monk went to the head monk to ask him about this, pointing out that if there were an error in the first copy, that error would be continued in all of the subsequent copies.

The head monk said, "We have been copying from the copies for centuries, but you make a good point, my son." So, he went down into the cellar with one of the copies to check it against the original. Hours passed and nobody saw him.

After a considerable amount of time passed, one of the monks went downstairs to look for him. He heard sobbing coming from the back of the cellar. He soon found the old monk leaning over one of the original books, crying. He asked the old monk what was wrong, and in a choked voice came the reply, "The word is '*celebrate*!'"

A WOMAN was trying hard to get the ketchup to come out of the jar. During her struggle the phone rang, so she asked her four-year-old daughter to answer the phone.

"It's the priest, mommy," the child said to her mother. Then she spoke into the phone, "Mommy can't come to the phone to talk to you right now. She's hitting the bottle."

THREE IRISH Catholic women stop across the street from a brothel.

"Isn't that Reverend Brown coming out of there?"

"What a scandal! For a clergyman to sink like that!"

"Isn't that Rabbi Farbstein?"

"Oh, that filthy man! Disgusting!"

"Isn't that Father Murphy?"

"My, my, there must be a very sick girl in there."

SEVERAL FRIARS were behind on their belfry payments so they opened up a small florist shop to raise funds.

Since everyone liked to buy flowers from the men of God, a rival florist across town thought the competition was unfair. He asked the good fathers to close down, but they would not. He went back some time later and begged the friars to close.

They ignored him.

So, the rival florist hired Hugh MacTaggart, the roughest and most vicious thug in town to "persuade" them to close. Hugh beat up the friars and trashed their store, saying he'd be back if they didn't close the shop.

Terrified, they did so, thereby proving that Hugh, and only Hugh, can prevent florist friars.

ROMAN CATHOLIC boy to Jewish boy: "Our parish priest knows more than your rabbi."

Jewish boy: "Of course he does. You tell him everything!"

A PRIEST was called away for an emergency. Not wanting to leave the confessional unattended, he called his rabbi friend from across the street and asked him to cover for him. The rabbi told him he wouldn't know what to say, but the priest told him to come on over and he'd stay with him for a little bit and show him what to do.

The rabbi came and he and the priest entered the confessional.

Within a few minutes, a woman came in and said "Father, forgive me for I have sinned."

The priest asked, "What did you do?"

The woman said, "I committed adultery."

Priest: "How many times?"

Woman: Three times."

Priest: "Say two Hail Marys, put $5 in the box and go and sin no more."

A few minutes later a man entered the confessional. He said, "Father, forgive me for I have sinned."

Priest: "What did you do?"

Man: "I committed adultery."

Priest: "How many times?"

Man: "Three times."

Priest: "Say two Hail Marys and put $5 in the box and go and sin no more."

The rabbi told the priest that he had the hang of it, so the priest left. A few minutes later another woman entered and said "Father, forgive me for I have sinned."

Rabbi: "What did you do?"

Woman: "I committed adultery."

Rabbi: "How many times?"

Woman: "Once."

Rabbi: "Go do it two more times. We have a special this week: three for $5."

A MAN walked to the top of a hill and talked to God.

"God, what's a million years to you?"

"A minute."

"What's a million dollars to you?"

"A penny."

"God, can I have a million dollars?"

"Sure . . . in a minute."

I heard this joke while attending Mass at St. Pius X Church in Charlottetown, P.E.I., on January 9, 2000:

TWO AMERICAN priests visited a church in Germany. They didn't speak German, and therefore wouldn't know what was going on, so they wondered what they should do. They saw a good-looking young man. "Let's sit behind him and do what he does."

During the Mass, the priest made an announcement and the young man stood up. The two priests did, also. The rest of the congregation remained seated, and laughed.

Later, the two American priests learned that the priest announced there would be a baptism and would the father of the baby please stand.

P.E.I. must be a hotbed of church laughter. My cousin, Brendon McCloskey, a Charlottetown city councillor for more than fourteen years, heard this one at Mass, from the priest at his local church, in spring 2002:

AN OLD country farmer with serious financial problems bought a mule from another farmer for $100. The seller agreed to deliver the mule the next day.

However, the next day he drove up and said, "I'm sorry, but I have some bad news. The mule died."

"Okay," said the second farmer. "Just give me my money back."

"Can't do that. I spent it already."

"Okay, just unload the mule here."

"What ya gonna do with a dead mule?"

"I'm going to raffle him off."

"You can't raffle off a dead mule!"

"Sure I can. I just won't tell anybody he's dead."

A month later, the two met up and the first farmer asked, "Whatever happened with the dead mule?"

"I raffled him off just like I said I would. I sold 500 tickets at $2 apiece and made a profit of $898."

"Didn't anybody complain?"

"Just the guy who won. So I gave him back his $2."

CHAPTER SEVEN

"The more you're scared, the more you have to create jokes."

Dominique Moisi

I have written hundreds of articles in my thirty-one-year-career as a corporate journalist, newspaper columnist, and magazine writer. Some of my favourite stories dealt with humour and laughter—even the following, which was about life, death and laughter:

Heaven's a Riot
Now Punster Pettit is Here

*By Dennis McCloskey (*Toronto Star*, August 21, 1997)*

A friend and former colleague died on Aug. 6 at 6:58 a.m. I'm sorry, but I just can't wipe the smile off my face.

It's okay. Bob would understand.

Bob Pettit was a graphic artist who enjoyed his job when he was employed in his chosen field but loathed work when it didn't involve his first love—layout and design.

Bob and I worked together for several years on a corporate magazine, but it wasn't until he took early retirement in 1986 that I got to know a hidden part of him. He was one of the wittiest and punniest people I have known.

In the last few years before his death, at age seventy, he taught me that far too many people die before they expire. "Why do we take life so seriously?" he once asked me. "After all, it's not permanent."

Bob revelled in early morning solitary walks near his Cobourg, Ontario, condominium along the shore of nearby Lake Ontario, which he shared with his wife, Betty. He marvelled, with child-like fascination—even in sickness—at the bright, rising sun. He even seemed to view his impending death with some levity.

Two weeks before he died, I spoke to him on the phone and he made me laugh harder and longer in twenty minutes than some people have in their lifetime.

He was suffering with cancer in his remaining lung and it had spread to his brain. He'd suffered a mild stroke, lost his balance and was in a wheelchair. "I don't think I'm going to be here much longer," he said. "So, I don't buy green bananas."

On the day he died, Betty called me to say he kept joking and punning almost to the end.

He wasn't all that lucid but at one point he brightened, looked up at Betty and spoke his final words on this earth, "Boy, that was funny!"

She has no idea what he was thinking and admits it is going to drive her crazy, wondering what was so funny. Later, I mentioned it to a friend and she suggested that perhaps God told him a joke just before he died.

It has been said that the only true dead are those who have been forgotten. Bob will be remembered most by those who were invited into the inner circle of his sharp wit.

On the day of his passing, Betty and I recalled some of his best and worst puns and we laughed until we cried. She remembered the day while driving on a country road they passed a herd of cows standing together in a field of corn. "They're having a cornference," Bob deadpanned. "They must be airing their beefs."

The last time I visited Bob, he told me about his volunteer work at the local hospital where he was in charge of the information desk. Everything he needed to know about the hospital was kept in a folder in the top drawer of his tiny desk. He said it made him a Top Drawer Executive. When the hospital obtained a fish tank, Bob was placed in charge of feeding the school of fish. During my visit to his home, he asked me to help him choose a title because he didn't think "*Fish Convenor*" was appropriate for a man of his age and station in life. He considered "*School Principal*" and even toyed with the idea of "*Sturgeon General*," adding that he could pad his résumé by saying he was a graduate of McGILL. The title we decided on that day stuck with him to the end. Among the hospital volunteers and staff, he would forever be known as "*The Codfather*."

Writers and poets get it wrong when they say there is no humour in heaven because the secret source of humour itself is not joy but sorrow.

When Bob's death was explained to his then four-year-old grandson, Zack, the tiny lad was told that when people die the rest of us could see them in things that sparkle—like stars, or light shining on the water. Shortly after that simplistic explanation, a prism in Betty's kitchen was accidentally jostled and the reflected light danced and cascaded throughout the room.

Bob's grandson shouted, "Look! Grandpa's happy!"

You bet he is.

* * * * * * * * * *

When I was passing around the collection plate, looking for jokes from priests, a few of them asked how I got into the business of writing. The long answer appears in my non-fiction book And Now, A Word From a Freelance Writer *(General Store Publishing House, 1993, 116 pages, $12.95). A much shorter version is reprinted here, if anyone's interested:*

Fear No More, Says the Heart Fear No More, Says the Soul

*By Dennis McCloskey (*Canadian Messenger, *November 1999)*

He had a face like a benediction.
Miguel De Cervantes

The temperature in downtown Toronto at noon on Thursday, November 20, 1980, was a chilly four degrees Celsius. A wet snow was falling as I walked northward on the east side of Yonge Street at 11:55 a.m. Ahead of me, two young boys spoke dejectedly of the previous night's NHL hockey game in which the Leafs were defeated 5–4 by archrival Les Canadiens, who extended their string of undefeated games to six. I glanced in the window of a record store and saw that a Barry Manilow LP record was selling for $4.49.

Why would I recall such trivial things on one particular day nearly two decades ago?

Well, why *wouldn't* I? My life changed on that day as I walked the short distance from the high-rise office building where I worked on King Street to the quiet solitude of a noon-hour Mass at St. Michael's Cathedral on nearby Church Street. I recall the day as though it were yesterday.

As I neared Richmond Street, my mind was not focused on cold weather, sports or music. I was in the midst of a mood-altering career crisis that was clouding my mind. I held what I considered to be one of the best jobs in my field, as editor of a national corporate magazine for one of the world's top companies, General Electric. But, inside, I felt empty and unfulfilled. My dream was to work on my own as a home-based freelance writer, yet I did not have the courage to escape from the corporate jungle. My heart was deeply troubled because I was afraid to make that terrifying leap from the security of a company job to the uncertainties of life as a freelancer. I had the unflinching support of my wife, Kris, but even her love and encouragement wasn't the catalyst I needed to strengthen my resolve to pursue my life's aspiration.

On that bleak and nippy day of November 20, the sidewalks were teeming with noonday shoppers, businesspeople ducking into restaurants for a quick lunch, and the usual phalanx of panhandlers and other street people who are a regular fixture on this section of the country's longest and most famous street. Lost as I was in my troubled thoughts, it was easy to ignore the blank, expressionless faces in the crowd. Even when a tall, bearded young man thrust a small booklet into my gloved hand, I didn't miss a stride.

However, even in my haste, I noticed there was something different about this shabbily dressed person who wore a long, dark-coloured raincoat that seemed much too flimsy to ward off the November chill. Our eyes met for the briefest of moments and he smiled at me. Unlike the other vagrants, he did not ask for money nor did he speak. It is said that the eyes are the windows of the soul and, upon reflection, it seemed like he was peering into the antiquity of my fearful soul.

I thought no more of this stranger and soon reached the cathedral just as the Mass started, at the regular time of 12:10 p.m. For me, St. Michael's served as an oasis, a respite from the maddening and dizzying pace that is set by the multitudes outside this magnificent building that has welcomed troubled hearts and doleful souls for 150 years.

During the service I prayed for guidance, strength and the courage to change my life and follow my dream. While the solitude of the cavernous church helped ease the pounding of my heart and quieted my mind somewhat, I was no more certain about my future when I left that calm edifice than when I had entered.

I stood on the steps of the church and steeled myself to rejoin the confusions of the day, my life and the city. I reached into a pocket for my gloves, and my hand came upon the tiny booklet that was handed to me by the stranger who spoke only with his eyes. For the first time, I saw that it was a miniature, red-covered, thirty-two-page Personal Bible measuring a mere 2" by 2.5". I opened it to the first page and read aloud the words of John 14:27 that filled the entire page. "*Let not your heart be troubled, neither let it be afraid.*" The verse rang in my ears like the tolling of a bell and I realized it was tolling for me.

It is difficult to describe the incredible feeling when a huge burden is suddenly lifted from the mind. It was as though I had been touched by an angel and God had intervened in my life during my time of despair. I quickly retraced my steps along Yonge Street but the man who'd given me the pamphlet was no longer there.

I know there is a great flutter of interest in angels these days, as the angel phenomenon takes on worldwide proportions, but angelic presence is not unique to this generation. It is as old as Christendom, and on a wintry day in November 1980, I am certain that an angel was sent to the corner of Yonge and Richmond Streets, in downtown Toronto, to give me the comfort and strength I needed to change my life.

I immediately returned to my office and resigned from my job. The very next morning, I made a "cold call" to the late Mike Walton, an editor at *The Toronto Star*, and said I had some story ideas that might interest him. He liked one of my suggestions and—to my astonishment and delight—offered to pay me $175 to write an article for the paper's Life Section. I was now a bona fide freelance writer.

Today, six books and several hundred newspaper and magazine articles later, I am still living my dream as an independent writer-for-hire.

If it were not for my Angel of Yonge Street, I would not be writing this story.

CHAPTER EIGHT

"A leader without a sense of humour is apt to be like the grass mower at the cemetery—he has lots of people under him, but nobody is paying him any attention."

Bob Ross

Father Thomas R. (Dave) Harding

St. Monica's
Toronto, Ontario

The final chapter of this book is dedicated to my friend and mentor, Father "Dave" Harding.

Father Dave Harding agrees that his late brother and best friend, Father Bill Harding, was, is, and always will be one of God's favourite Jesters. Dave refers to himself as "the brother of one of the greatest storytellers of all" and acknowledges that Bill must be getting lots of laughs in heaven with the likes of Charlie Chaplin, The Marx Brothers, Laurel & Hardy, The Three Stooges, Wayne & Shuster and others—all competing for God's attention and laughter.

If you read Chapter One on Father Bill, you might agree with Father Dave's assessment of his younger brother. But you have to know the second half of the Harding Boys before you can make that judgment. Father Dave once told his brother-priest, "I have read your joke books and I have read your serious books. The serious ones are funnier than the joke books!"

Father Dave is perhaps best known and loved for his self-deprecating wit but he also revels in telling funny stories he's heard from others. He tells of a time he and his brother were playing golf, and a friend, Sean Evelyn, told them, "You priests are doing a great job around here. I keep hearing the name of your boss mentioned all over the course. Trouble is, it's not being mentioned in prayer!"

Dave remembers his sibling as "a tremendous brother, a sparkling companion, a good sport, an Irish tenor, the most generous person you could ever meet, a gentleman and a scholar, the greatest guy in the world, and in my humble and prejudiced opinion, the best pastor I ever met." Father Dave chuckles at the memory of his brother's sometimes-irreverent humour, often at the good-natured expense of the church hierarchy. He gives one example: Father Bill got to know Archbishop Jorge Urosa, of Valencia, Venezuela, when Urosa studied at Toronto's St. Augustine's Seminary and later, as a deacon, when he was sent to Annunciation Parish in Don Mills to assist Father Bill. Years later, as he rose through the ranks of the Catholic Church, Archbishop

Urosa's Episcopal motto became "*Pro Mundi Vita.*" ("For the life of the world.") Father Bill would say to him, "Pro Mundi Vita. Pro Tuesday Vita. Pro Wednesday Vita."

Fathers Bill and Dave often served as grist for my mill as a writer. The following is an article I wrote about the two punny priests that was published at the turn of the century:

The Merchants of Faith (and Mirth)

By Dennis McCloskey

*(*Good Times Magazine, Ontario Gazette*, January 2000)*

IT WAS William Shakespeare who told us that all the world's a stage and we are merely players with our exits and entrances. In *As You Like It*, the bard noted, "One man in his time plays many parts." If only he'd known Bill and Dave Harding, he might have revised his prose to add that two can play this game. As it was, he must have been thinking of a pair of mischievous priests like the Harding brothers when he penned, "Double, double, toil and trouble" in *Macbeth*. "Our sense of humour sometimes got us into trouble," says Father Dave, the eighty-one-year-old retired Toronto priest, who declined to provide specific examples, except to say, "sometimes you have to be a little crazy to be sane."

He describes himself as "the needler," while the late Father Bill was the humorist who "went for the shock effect."

Thomas R. "Dave" Harding was born on October 18, 1918, five years before his brother, Bill, entered the stage. For the next seventy-one years, the brothers would become almost inseparable, until Bill made his final exit on September 12, 1994. (Another brother, Jack, is also deceased and there is a stepsister, Jane, and a stepbrother, Tom, who was a foreign missionary priest in Japan for thirty years before his retirement.)

Dave was ordained a Roman Catholic priest in 1942, and Bill entered the priesthood six years later. In the next seven decades, the brothers would positively affect the lives of untold thousands of people and become known as church builders. Between them, they founded three churches in the Toronto area (Annunciation, Holy Spirit and Prince of Peace). They also became widely known and affectionately regarded for their quick wit and good humour. While Father Bill served in six parishes during his forty-six-year career as a priest, Father Dave endured more than nineteen assignments "because I kept trying to tell the boss how to run the parish," he jokes. During that time, the pair interspersed their priestly lives with world travel and adventures that included flying their own Cessna 150s in tandem; riding horses in B.C.; hunting in Northern Ontario; skiing in Banff; hiking on Baffin Island; golfing at Old St. Andrew's in Scotland; and entering and winning tennis tournaments.

Their down-to-earth wit and wisdom was much loved and appreciated by parishioners, in particular, but the brothers captured the hearts and favour of people of all faiths. At golf tournaments, Father Bill would be asked to be in charge of arranging good weather—because of his supposed direct line to God—but he would decline, saying he was "in sales, not management." Another time, he roasted a retiring priest by calling him a man of rare gifts. "He rarely gives any," he deadpanned.

All of this and more are contained in a ninety-three-page book written in 1996 by Father Dave, to commemorate the life of his younger brother and business and travelling companion. "I didn't think he got the proper credit for all he had done," says the author, who has an Honours B.A., a Master's Degree in Philosophy, and a PhD in Education from the University of Toronto. "Writing the book was good therapy. I would recommend such a project to anyone grieving for a loved one." He printed 500 copies of the book, entitled *William F. Harding, Parish Priest*, and gave them all away. It's just one of nine books written by the unpretentious Father Dave, who was Professor of Philosophy at Scarborough's St. Augustine's Seminary in 1946. Not to be outdone, Father Bill (who had two Master's degrees and a doctorate) also published nine books, including a joke book entitled *Har-Dee-Har-Har*.

Father Dave says he is not very successful at retiring. He serves as priest in residence at St. Monica's Parish in Toronto, giving occasional sermons and hearing confessions, and he fills in when needed at other churches in the diocese. "There is a shortage of priests, and the church could respond to this need by calling more on retired priests like me," he suggests.

When asked to outline his philosophy of life and how he wants to be remembered, Father Dave says he believes in hard work and caring for everything and everybody. "I would just like to be remembered. I don't care how," he adds with a twinkle in his eye.

* * * * * * * * * * *

Just before the occasion of the sixtieth anniversary of his ordination to the priesthood, on May 30, 2002, I asked Father Dave if he would contribute some of his favourite jokes and stories to my book. He said he would be pleased, because he sees and enjoys humour in the commonplace of everyday life. "Humour is all about us, every day of our lives," he said. "And thank God for that!" He added, "If you keep smiling and laughing through your tears of joy and sorrow, people won't know what you are up to."

He recounted several funny stories and anecdotes but he did more than that. He also added a cerebral touch to this book by writing a serious essay on the Humour of Jesus Christ, G.K. Chesterton, William Shakespeare, and the late Jesuit philosopher Father Bernard Lonergan. Following are samples of some of his favourite jokes that he has collected from friends and colleagues:

THE ELDER priest, speaking to the younger priest, said, "I know you were reaching out to the young people when you had bucket seats installed in the church to replace the first four pews. And it worked. The front of the church gets filled up first."

The young priest nodded and the elderly one continued, "And, you said that a little more beat to the music would bring young people back to the church, so I supported you when you brought in that rock 'n' roll gospel choir. Even the balcony became packed with church-goers."

"So, what's the problem?" asked the young priest.

"Well," said the elder priest. "I'm afraid you've gone too far with the drive-thru confessional."

"But Father," protested the young priest. "My confessions have nearly doubled since I began that!"

"I know, my son, but the flashing '*Toot 'n' Tell or Go to Hell*' neon sign has to go!"

A TORONTO motorist was becoming more and more frustrated as he unsuccessfully tried find a downtown parking space so he could keep an important appointment and save his job.

Finally, in desperation, he parked his car illegally and left the following note on the windshield of his car: "Officer, I have been circling this block for 20 minutes in search of a parking spot. If I don't keep my appointment, I will lose my job. Forgive us our trespasses." Sincerely, J. Smith.

A police officer arrived and wrote out a parking ticket. He left it on the windshield of the car with the following note: "Dear J. Smith: I have been circling this block for 20 years. If I don't give you a ticket, I'll lose my job. Lead us not into temptation." Sincerely, Officer Brown.

FOLLOWING A church service on Sunday morning, a young boy suddenly announced to his mother, "Mom, I've decided to become a priest when I grow up."

"That's fine with me and your father, but what made you decide that?" his mother asked.

"Well," said the little boy. "I have to go to church on Sunday anyway, and I figure it will be more fun to stand up and yell than to sit and listen."

A SIX-YEAR-OLD was overheard reciting the Lord's Prayer at Mass: "And forgive us our trash passes, as we forgive those who passed trash against us."

A BOY was watching his father, a minister, write a sermon. "How do you know what to say?" he asked.

"Why, God tells me."

"Oh, then why do you keep crossing things out?"

A LITTLE girl became restless as the priest's homily dragged on and on. Finally, she leaned over to her mother and whispered, "Mommy, if we give him the money now, will he let us go?"

AN AIRPLANE was about to crash. There were three parachutes on board and four passengers: a married man, a politician, a student, and an elderly priest. The first passenger said, "I am a married man with three children. My family cannot live without me." So, he grabbed a parachute and jumped.

The second passenger said, "I am an important politician. I have great responsibilities and a lot of people rely on my intelligence and good judgment." So, he strapped on a parachute and jumped.

That left the student and the elderly priest.

The priest turned to the student and said, "I have lived a long and happy life. You are young, with your life before you. You may have the last parachute."

"That won't be necessary," said the student. "The politician has taken my school backpack."

EPILOGUE

Harding on Humour

When I asked Father Dave Harding if he would consider contributing a few words for the Epilogue of *God's Jesters*, the philosopher priest penned a literary composition on humour. He wrote that artists, historically, have depicted Jesus Christ as a melancholy, sad, severe person but he argued this is not the case. "I believe he was a very cheerful person because he was always in demand," he wrote. "He was the life of the party, and children flocked to Him. Children usually avoid sour people."

He quoted G.K. Chesterton—the English journalist, novelist, poet, and critic—who wrote, "Joy is the gigantic secret of the Christian." And Father Dave is in total agreement with Chesterton when the late author speaks of the "mirth" and sense of humour of Jesus. "Perhaps Jesus went into the mountains, not only to pray, but to have a good, hearty laugh with the Father and the Holy Spirit about some of the amusing individuals or to share the latest jokes about the humans on earth," said Father Dave.

A former philosophy teacher, Father Dave considers Father Bernard J. Lonergan, S.J. (1904–84) to be one of the two greatest theologians of the twentieth century (the other, he says, is Karl Rahner) and he quoted both men in his essay-like comments for *God's Jesters*. Father Dave pointed to one of Lonergan's twenty books, *Insight: A Study of Human Understanding*, in which the Canadian Jesuit philosopher and theologian had this to say about humour and satire: "Satire laughs *at*; humour laughs *with*. Satire would depict the counter positions in their current, concrete features and by that serene act of cool objectification it would hurry them to their destiny of bringing about their own reversal. In contrast, humour keeps the positions in contact with human limitations and human infirmity . . . for if satire becomes red with indignation, humour blushes with humility."

He continued to quote Lonergan, "For as satire can help man swing out of the self-centredness of an animal in a habitat to the universal viewpoint of an intelligent human being, so humour can aid him to the discovery of the complex problem of grasping and holding the nettle of a restricted, effective freedom."

Father Dave said he prefers the charitable approach of humour to the harsh treatment of satire. "I would rather laugh with someone than to laugh at them in the pursuit of knowledge as well as in the attaining of goodness."

He ended his piece by writing about the greatest writer of all—William Shakespeare, whom Harding described as "The Great Bard who was the Master of Comedies and Tragedies." (Father Dave noted that a comedy is a stage play of light, amusing, and often satirical character—chiefly representing everyday life and with a happy ending—while a tragedy is defined as drama in prose or verse of elevated theme and diction and with an unhappy ending.)

"It is rather surprising that while Shakespeare's Tragedies are better known, he wrote more comedies (fourteen) than tragedies (thirteen)," wrote Father Dave, whose favourite Shakespearian play, at Stratford, was *A Midsummer Night's Dream*, starring Irish actress Siobhan McKenna.

Father Dave suggested that lovers of comedy should read one or all of Shakespeare's comedies. Forsooth, in a parting gesture (Jester?) he listed them all: *The Tempest; The Two Gentlemen of Verona; The Merry Wives of Windsor; Measure for Measure; Comedy of Errors; Much Ado about Nothing; Love's Labours Lost; A Midsummer Night's Dream; The Merchant of Venice; As You Like It; The Taming of the Shrew; Twelfth Night; The Winter's Tale; and . . .*

. . . *All's Well That Ends Well.*

ABOUT THE AUTHOR

Dennis McCloskey is a full-time freelance writer. Since graduating from Ryerson with a journalism degree in 1971, he has worked as a corporate journalist and editor, newspaper columnist, magazine writer, and book author. Hundreds of his human interest and business articles have appeared in more than sixty newspapers, consumer publications and trade magazines in Canada, the United States and Europe. This is his sixth book. He lives in Richmond Hill, Ontario, with his wife, Kris, a retired high-school teacher.

To order more copies of

GOD'S JESTERS

Humour from the Pulpit

send $15.95 plus $6.00

to cover GST, shipping and handling to:

GENERAL STORE PUBLISHING HOUSE

Box 28, 1694B Burnstown Road

Burnstown, Ontario Canada K0J 1G0

Telephone: 1-800-465-6072

Fax: (613) 432-7184

www.gsph.com

VISA and MASTERCARD accepted